ANCESTORS GODDESSES AND HEROES

SCULPTURES FROM ASIA, AFRICA AND EUROPE

Deutscher Kunstverlag

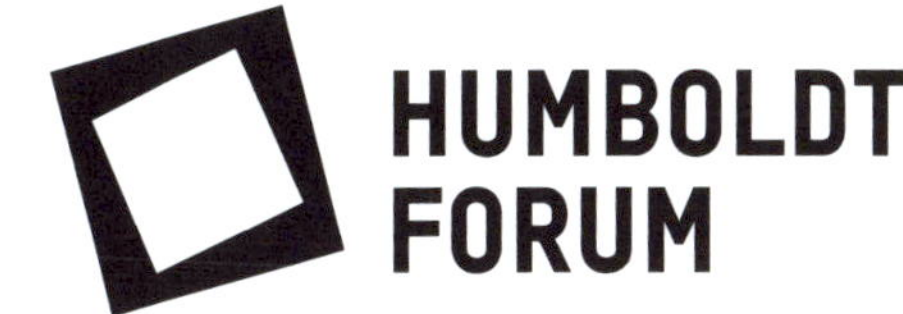

CONTENTS

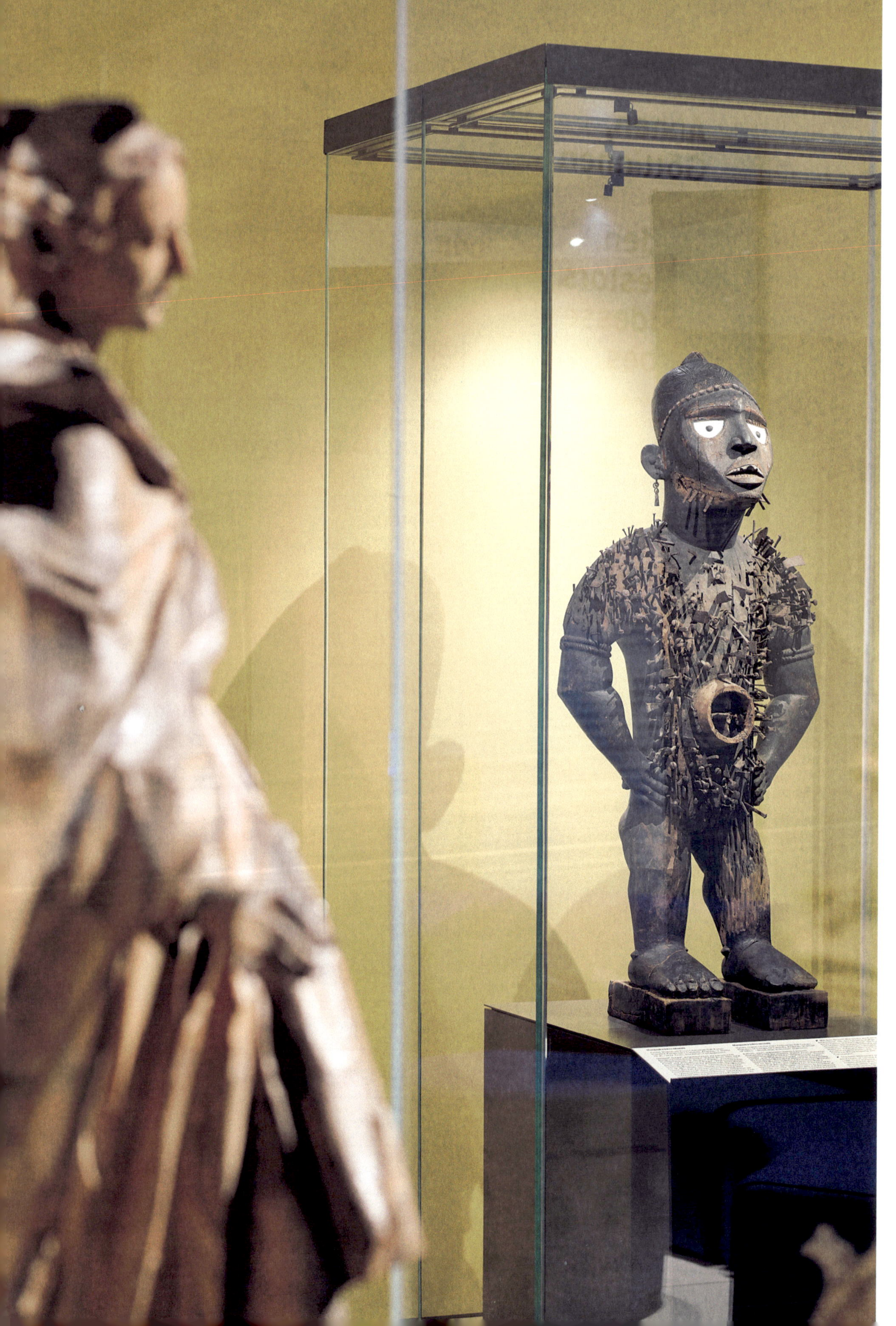

FOREWORD

Hartmut Dorgerloh and Lars-Christian Koch

What connects the forty-five visibly heterogeneous objects assembled here in the Humboldt Forum's temporary exhibition *ANCESTORS, GODDESSES AND HEROES?* What is the common thread, the conceptual category, that for all their differences, they all share? Is this equating of the unequal not just a flight of fancy – an idea adopted from a great distance? ————

Well, let's find out, first by moving closer and then by taking a step back. What first catches the eye is just how unalike the selected works are. They were created in completely different periods ranging between the third and the nineteenth century, and in vastly different cultural spheres spread over three continents, namely Central Africa, East Asia and Western Europe. Never before have they been seen in this particular constellation. ————

So what, stepping back to view them from a greater distance, are their points in common? Three of these can be named, although there are probably many more. First, all the objects come from Berlin collections, namely those of the Ethnologisches Museum, the Skulpturensammlung and the Museum für Byzantinische Kunst der Staatlichen Museen zu Berlin; second, they are united by their erstwhile function, since every one of them was born of the universal human need for protection, guidance and security; third, they share the same fate in that they are all 'orphaned' ritual objects that have been removed – often by force – from their original functional context. ————

Instead, these figures have become museum exhibits for us viewers to look at, and that our own encounter with them is motivated by interests and expectations very different from those of their makers goes without saying. So how do these mute ritual objects engage with us as people of the twenty-first century? What can they tell us about their origins and the transformations they have undergone? Have they retained any of their original powers? Or are they simply precious artifacts? Are they images or icons? Heroes or intermediaries? ————

The temporary exhibitions staged by the Stiftung Humboldt Forum im Berliner Schloss in collaboration with the Staatliche Museen zu Berlin and other partners turn the spotlight on the transcendent aspects of the cultural spheres in which we operate. *ANCESTORS, GODDESSES AND HEROES: SCULPTURES FROM ASIA, AFRICA AND EUROPE* is a joint project by a cross-institutional team of curators from the Ethnologisches Museum, the Skulpturensammlung and the Museum für Byzantinische Kunst, both of the Staatliche Museen zu Berlin, and the Stiftung Humboldt Forum im Berliner Schloss, to all of whom we extend our sincerest thanks. ————

We now have the pleasure of inviting you to view these forty-five emissaries of distant times and cultures and to let them steer your thoughts into illuminating new realms.

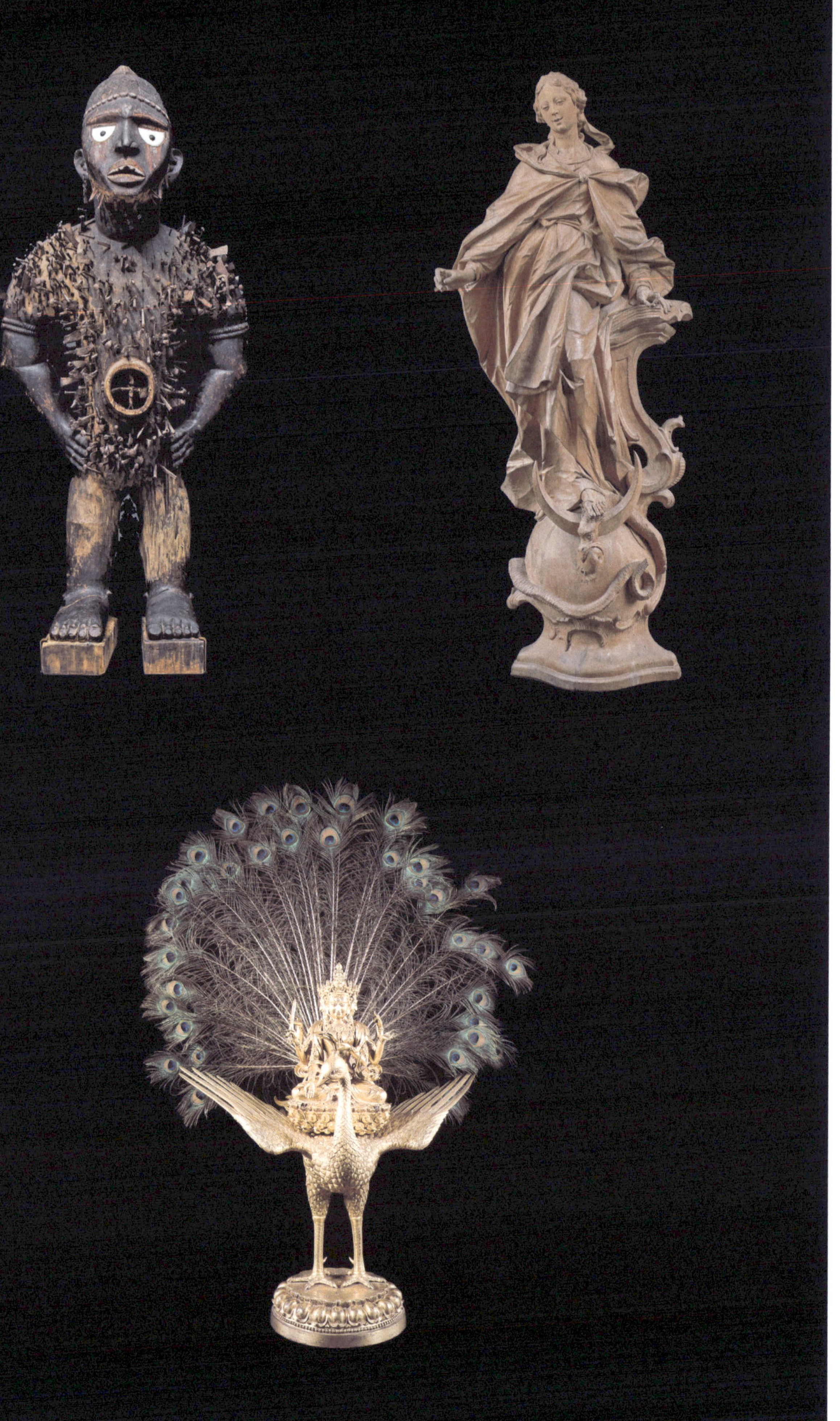

INTRODUCTION

**Tanja-Bianca Schmidt, Nathalie Küchen,
Barbara Lenz**

ANCESTORS, GODDESSES AND HEROES shows selected works of art from Central Africa, East Asia and Western Europe exhibited alongside each other for the first time. Despite the obvious differences between them, the works are united by one fundamental aspect: they all played a key role in cultural practices and were central to overcoming both individual and societal crises. They stand for the presumed existence of an invisible world of gods, spirits and ancestors, and helped forge a palpable link between this world and a 'different reality'. Through the powers ascribed to them, they provided security and guidance, averted perils and punished rule breakers. They enlisted the intercession of ancestors, divine beings or the 'one true God', or were a source of inspiration at the personal level. ⸺

MANGAAKA, MAHAMAYURI AND MARY IMMACULATE STANDING ON THE EARTH

The exhibition's three key works demonstrate the unshakeable conviction with which people of different periods and on different continents invested sculptural figures with the power to protect, heal or punish. ⸺

To the communities living along the Loango coast in today's Democratic Republic of Congo and Angola, the sculpture from Africa, a *NKISI NKONDI*, was both a visible manifestation of *MANGAAKA*, or jurisdiction, and a concrete response to the ever greater threat posed by the European colonial powers. The Asian work, a *MAHAMAYURI*, is venerated from India to China, its place of origin, as the tutelary god that affords protection against natural disasters. The third work was created in eighteenth-century Europe and comes from a church in Bavaria. The iconography of its depiction of the *VIRGIN MARY* standing on the earth turns on the idea of freeing the world from original sin. Such Marian icons carry great emotional weight for millions of Christians, who derive hope and comfort from them to this day. ⸺

The forty-five exhibits dating from the fourth to the nineteenth century are drawn from three different Berlin collections belonging to the Staatliche Museen zu Berlin: the Ethnologisches Museum, the Skulpturensammlung and the Museum für Byzantinische Kunst der Staatliche Museen zu Berlin. The collective contemplation of such disparate works prompts a discussion that goes to the very heart of what institutions dedicated to collecting, preserving and categorising actually do, exposing the divisions that this exhibition seeks to transcend. ⸺

HOW NATURAL IS DIFFERENCE?

The study of these objects takes us deep into the early days of the Staatliche Museen zu Berlin, which began with the gradual dispersal of the Brandenburgisch-Preußische Kunstkammer and the reallocation of its holdings to the specialist museums founded by royal decree between 1830 and 1930. ⸺

The Königliches Museum (now the Altes Museum, Museumsinsel) that opened in 1830 was the first museum in Berlin to be open to people 'of all classes'.[1] It housed parts of the Brandenburg art collection, including numerous European paintings and sculptures. Most of these dated from Antiquity to the Renaissance and were judged to be 'high art' that warranted presentation in a building whose architecture combined stylistic elements from both periods. The carefully composed overview of art history provided by the galleries of this egalitarian educational institution served primarily to enable an aesthetic appreciation of the works and to foster in visitors a socially defined sense of taste. Closely bound up with this was the striving of the upwardly mobile middle classes to educate themselves and through art to train their intellectual powers of discrimination and discernment, as envisaged by Wilhelm von Humboldt. ⸺

Fig. 1–3 The three key figures in the exhibition *Ancestors, Goddesses and Heroes*

The Neues Museum, which is also located on the Museumsinsel and opened twenty years later in 1850, was intended to provide a counterweight to the art-historical bias of the neighbouring collection. In its eagerness to present a suggested cultural evolution of humanity from 1859 onwards for as broad an audience as possible, it exhibited items of relevance to the history of culture, including everyday objects, weaponry, textiles and 'ritual figures', and extrapolated from these a narrative that was erroneously premised on the existence of 'natural' differences between peoples based solely on skin colour, which in a sleight of hand was equated with the different stages of development so far reached. The presentation of cultural artifacts ultimately followed Friedrich Hegel's teleological view of history, meaning that visitors were led from the 'lower' to the 'higher' cultures, that is, from the Egyptian, prehistoric, and ethnological collections on the ground floor to the plaster casts of Ancient Greek and Roman sculpture and Europe's early modern period on the first floor. This powerful staging of a eurocentric view of history created the impression of a 'natural' hierarchical order with the 'white man' at the top, which of course was very useful to concurrent efforts to forge a national identity as well as supply a justification for colonialism. ———

Germany's colonial expansion, which entailed not only opening up new geographical regions and with them new markets and opportunities for trade, but also conceptualising what culture actually is or should be, reinforced the white Europeans' sense of their own cultural superiority. The structures established by colonial governments or even just diplomatic relations in the occupied territories also empowered colonial players on the ground. ————————

As ever more cultural creations from all over the world were amassed, so still more museums were built to house them. Amongst these was the Königliches Museum für Völkerkunde (now the Ethnologisches Museum) on Königgrätzerstrasse (now Stresemannstrasse) which opened in 1886 and provided space for both the prehistoric holdings and the now vastly enlarged ethnographic collection comprising works from Oceania, Africa, Mesoamerica and North America. Prior to its demolition in 1961, it stood in the immediate proximity of the Kunstgewerbemuseum (Museum of Arts and Crafts) that opened in 1881 in the purpose-built Martin-Gropius-Bau. The objects from East Asia, by contrast, were judged to be works of art, which led to the 1906 opening of the Ostasiatische Kunstsammlung. While this institution was initially housed in a partitioned-off section of the Völkerkundemuseum, in 1924 it was moved to permanent premises of its own on the ground floor of the Kunstgewerbemuseum. ————————————

The early days of the twentieth century saw the Museumsinsel endowed with yet another new building, the Kaiser-Friedrich-Museum (now the Bode-Museum). This housed many of the European paintings and post-antique sculptures from the Altes Museum, which it grouped together with craft objects, furnishings and architectural elements in tightly packed ensembles designed to evoke the mood of a particular epoch. Finally, the addition of the Pergamon Museum, which as of 1930 housed the collection of ancient architecture, the Department of the Ancient Near East, the Department of Islamic Art and the Deutsches Museum, turned the Museumsinsel into a storehouse of 'civilisation' that brought together works of art from Europe, the Mediterranean and Mesopotamia (now Iraq and north-eastern Syria).[2] ————————

What the museum concepts described here resolutely ignored was that the three continents from which the works were drawn, namely Africa, Asia and Europe, had been closely intertwined by trade relations, not least by the Trans-Saharan trade route that until 1590 linked West Africa to the Mediterranean, to name just one example. Ideas and religions followed the same routes as the commodities, reaching even very remote regions. Buddhism, for example, travelled along the Silk Road from India to China and Japan (115 BCE–13th cent.). In the

Fig. 4 Exhibition of the African Collection at the Königliches Museum für Völkerkunde at Königgrätzer Straße (today: Stresemannstraße) 120, corner of Prinz-Albrecht-Straße (today: Niederkirchnerstraße), photograph taken before 1926

Fig. 5 Exhibition of the Gemäldegalerie and Skulpturensammlung at the Kaiser-Friedrich-Museum, Room 36, Italian bronzes of the 16th century, photograph c. 1917

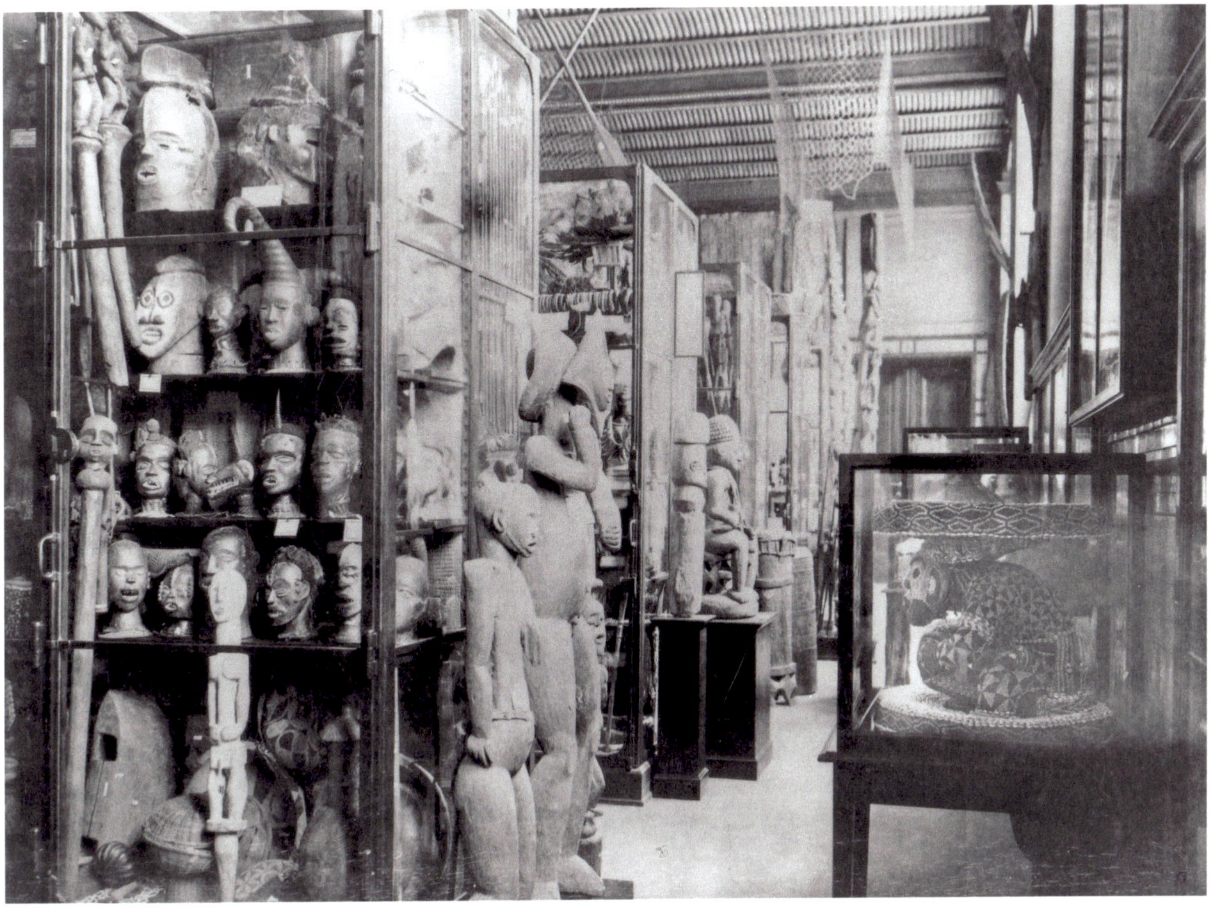

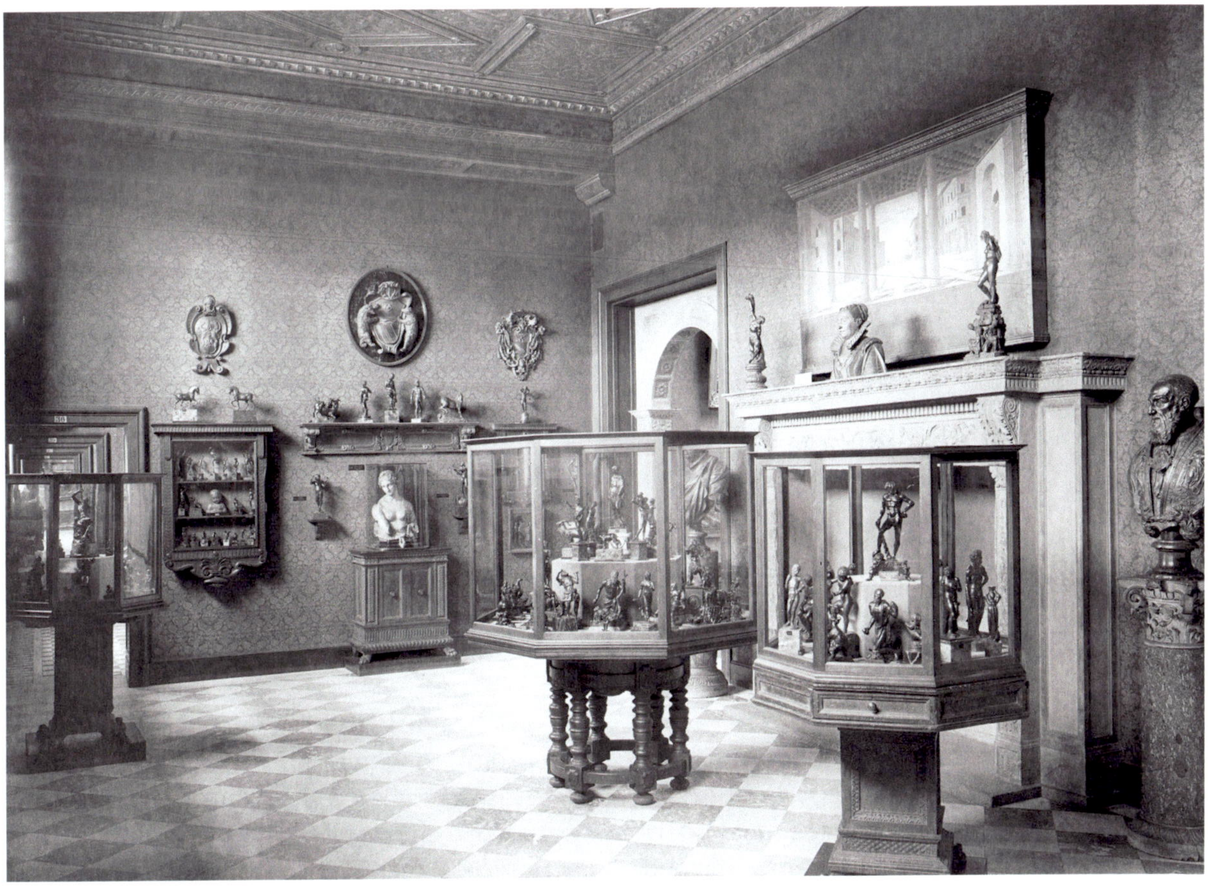

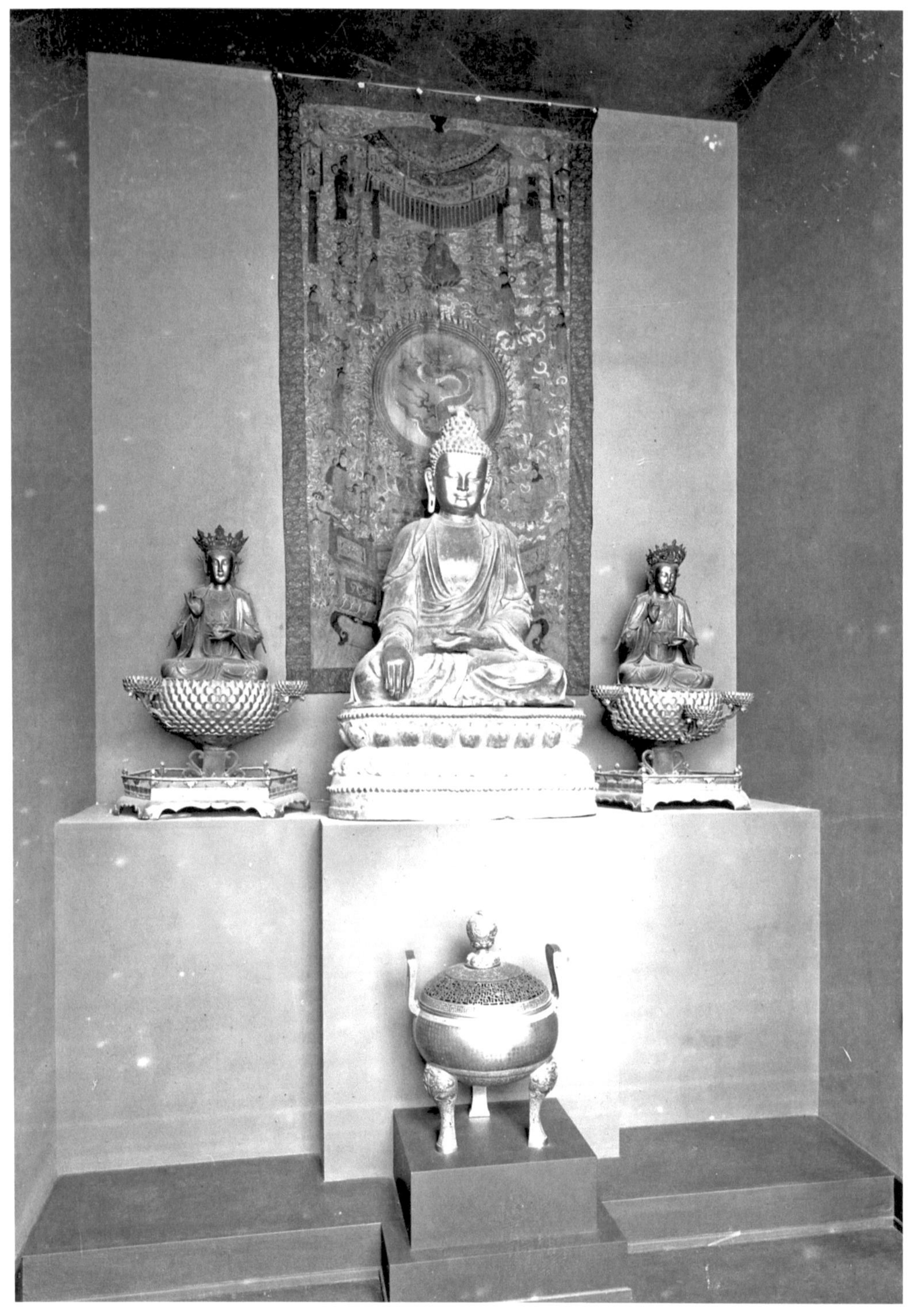

Fig. 6 Chinese Buddhism exhibition at the Ostasiatische Kunstsammlung at Prinz-Albrecht-Straße (today: Niederkirchnerstraße)

'universal collections', Kunstkammer and cabinets of curiosity amassed by the elites long before the advent of public museums, these long-standing ties had coalesced into models of a worldview that regarded nature, culture, art and science as different aspects of a single whole.[3] The vast collection of the Berliner Kunstkammer housed on the first floor of the Berliner Stadtschloss, for example, comprised an eclectic array of objects whose primary purpose was to demonstrate the encyclopaedic knowledge and global reach of the Brandenburg electors. That endeavour was supported by the principle of equivalence, according to which natural and artificial objects as well as everyday objects and utensils were to be shown alongside each other as of equal value. This idea of staging a supposedly universalising context for unequal things was nevertheless jettisoned at the founding of Berlin's first museums. ─────────

Museum exhibitions, which steer their audiences' attention, choreograph their visits, propose meanings, shape worldviews and dictate cultural concepts, can still be described as orderings of knowledge even today. In the past, our perception of non-European cultures was framed by a complex scholarly apparatus, whose quasi-evolutionary, social-Darwinist theories seeped deep into the social consciousness and influenced our worldview with lasting effect.[4] The spatial separation of objects enforced on the basis of seemingly objective criteria supported the dogmatic distinction between 'primitive' and 'civilised', which still informs the hierarchical perception of our material heritage propagated by many museums even now. Similarly consequential was the accentuation of cultural difference that would define perceptions of the 'other' right up to the present. Many of the holdings of Berlin's museums can be traced back to the far-reaching influence of the House of Brandenburg and have since then been steadily supplemented by works from other sources. In view of the ongoing criticism of the heritage of German colonialism housed in Berlin's museums, the Humboldt Forum believes it has a duty to address the value judgements and ideology that once underpinned the creation of the Berlin collections. ─────────

The exhibition *ANCESTORS, GODDESSES AND HEROES: SCULPTURES FROM ASIA, AFRICA AND EUROPE* can therefore be understood as an inquiry into the involvement and complicity of Berlin's museums in European colonialism. Tragically, the 'collection mania' that took hold of the upper echelons of society conflated the amassing of objects with the accumulation of knowledge and power. This motivated the systematic expansion of Berlin's museum collections in competition with some of the world's other great museums, such as those in London, Paris, Chicago and Detroit. What all the exhibits shown here share is the fact that their transformation into museum exhibits has decontextualised them and hence changed them in respect of both function and impact. Their 'acquisition' for the newly emergent museums of the nineteenth century was prompted by many factors and pursued with often highly dubious methods, with the result that their original authors and complex functional contexts are rarely documented. ─────────

Colonial players in far-away countries often took advantage of their power over indigenous peoples to loot countless objects that they then handed over – sometimes for a modest reward – as 'display objects' to the museums in Berlin. The works from Africa, for example, were added to the collection of the Ethnologisches Museum during the nineteenth and twentieth centuries, when Europe was busily laying claim to the world. ─────────

The exhibits from East Asia, many of them perceived as handicrafts in their place of origin,[5] began appearing on the international art market during the turmoil that marked the end of the Chinese empire and that culminated in the Xinhai Revolution of 1911 and the founding of the Chinese Republic (that existed from 1912–1949). Much sought-after by European collectors, these 'Far Eastern' artifacts, in German known as *Ostasiatika*, were eagerly snapped up as especially prestigious 'trophies'. Some of the exhibits originally belonged to private collections, parts of which were later purchased by Berlin's expanding museums. The two Buddha pupils from the estate of the collector Paul Wegener are a good example of this. ─────────

Some of the figures and objects from the Skulpturensammlung and the Museum für Byzantinische Kunst came to the museum as a result of the church's unstoppable loss of power and influence following the Reformation and Enlightenment – some of them by force, others as a result of changing tastes, for example within the ecclesiastical elite. ─────────

The exact circumstances under which most of the works shown here were acquired nevertheless remain obscure. Even those exhibits which from the point of view of the museum were lawfully accessioned at the time of their acquisition may yet turn out to have a dubious provenance. The Spanish *Pietà*, for example, was a gift of a former Nazi party member,

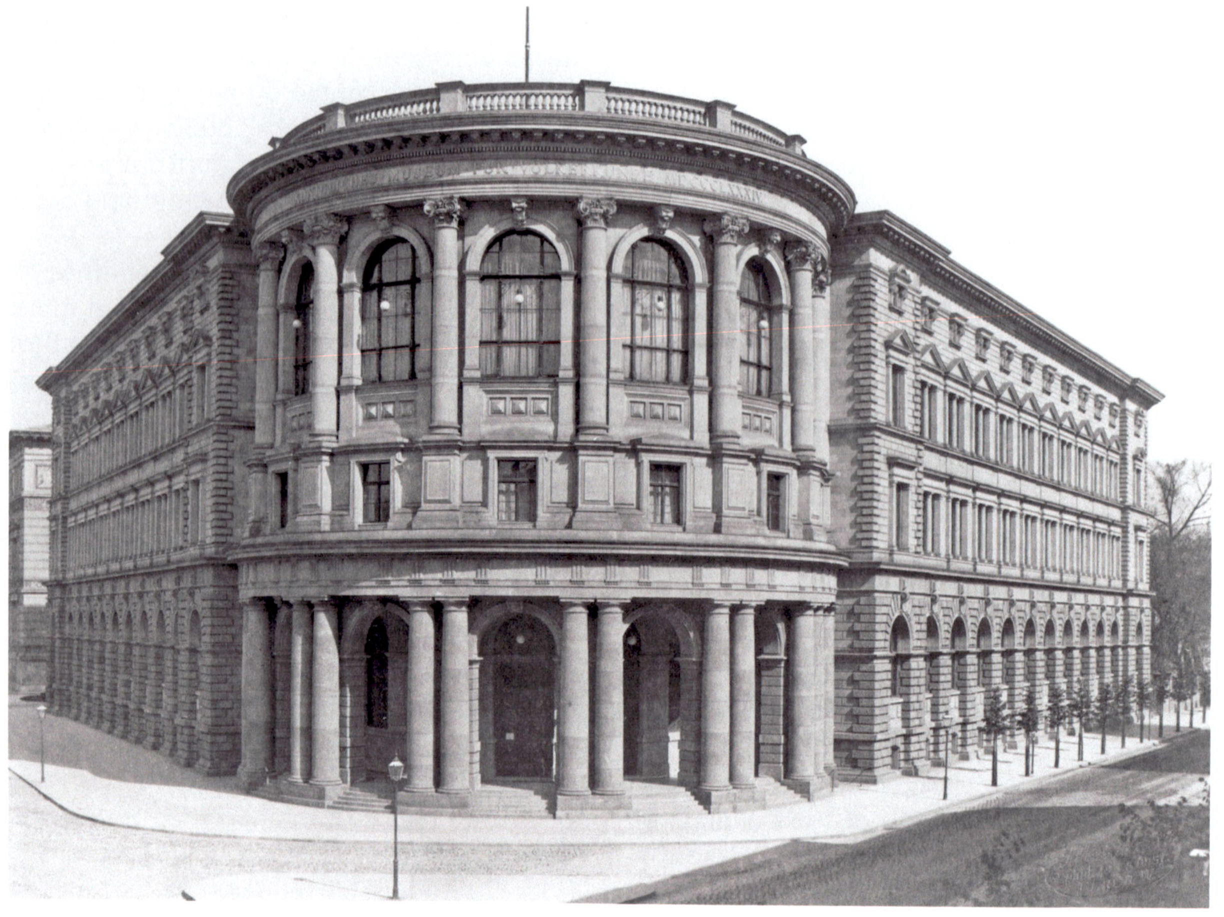

Fig. 7 The Königliches Museum für Völkerkunde, photograph taken before 1895

Franz Rademacher, yet we know neither where it came from nor how Rademacher came to be in possession of it |see pp. 62/63|. ———

Given the objects' complex religious, political, economic and social contexts, the question of what their original role might have been and what gaps they left behind when they were taken away must also be addressed. Notwithstanding how museums classify them, the works are neither 'merely' art nor are they 'merely' cultural artifacts. They are rather an amalgam of religion, politics, culture and aesthetics, and closely bound up with all of them.

The exhibits are presented in seven chapters titled 'What does "protection" actually mean?', 'How are evil forces kept in check?', 'Are they all genuine?', 'Can a word describe a thing?', 'Which image is an icon?', 'What is in a face?' and 'Are all heroes alike?' It is conceived, in other words, both as an invitation to question the thought patterns and value judgements impressed upon us by educational institutions such as museums and the media, and as a rejection of that narrative that disregards the commonalities and connections between geographically, historically and socially separate spheres. It also lays the groundwork for a sensory appreciation of the multiple worldviews on display. Our aim, in other words, was to make it possible for both areas of agreement and areas of difference to be experienced as an enrichment of our own perspective. ———

The exhibition and book would have been inconceivable without the debate over the Humboldt Forum's handling of its ethnographic collections. The sensitive and judicious use of any such terms as might reproduce stereotypical perceptions of the exhibited objects or encourage their categorisation as 'exotic' was a matter of the utmost importance to the authors – and not just when writing the texts. Clearly, it was vital that the descriptions of the works enable readers to grasp the complex interaction of aesthetics and function that each embodies. Hence the focus on the works' aesthetic properties as well as their conceptual content and at least one aspect of their function. It is therefore with great pleasure, and anticipation, that we invite viewers to pick up any, or all, of the many different threads provided and to follow them wherever they may lead.

1   Elisabeth Weisser-Lohmann, 'Das Nationalmuseum – Konzeptionen um 1800', in *Kunst als Kulturgut 2, '"Kunst und Staat"'*, ed. Annemarie Gethmann-Siefert, Bernadette Collenberg-Plotnikov and Elisabeth Weisser-Lohmann (Munich, 2011).

2   On the concept of 'Islamic art' see Wendy M. K. Shaw, *What is 'Islamic' Art? Between Religion and Perception* (Cambridge, 2019).

3   Gabriele Beßler, 'Kunst- und Wunderkammern', in *Europäische Geschichte Online (EGO)*, ed. Leibniz-Institut für Europäische Geschichte, 2015, http://ieg-ego.eu/de/threads/crossroads/wissensraeume/gabriele-bessler-kunstkammern-und-wunderkammern.

4   On the connection between museums and worldviews, see Tony Bennett, 'Ausstellung, Wahrheit, Macht: Ein Blick zurück auf den "Ausstellungskomplex"', in *Der documenta 14 Reader*, ed. Quinn Latimer and Adam Szymczyk (Munich/London/New York, 2017), pp. 339–352; see also Tony Bennett, 'Der bürgerliche Blick: Das Museum und die Organisation des Sehens', in *Die Ausstellung: Politik eines Rituals*, ed. Dorothea von Hantelmann and Carolin Meister (Zurich/Berlin, 2010), pp. 47–77.

5   The re-revaluation of the sculptures in Europe's museums has changed this way of seeing, especially over the past few decades.

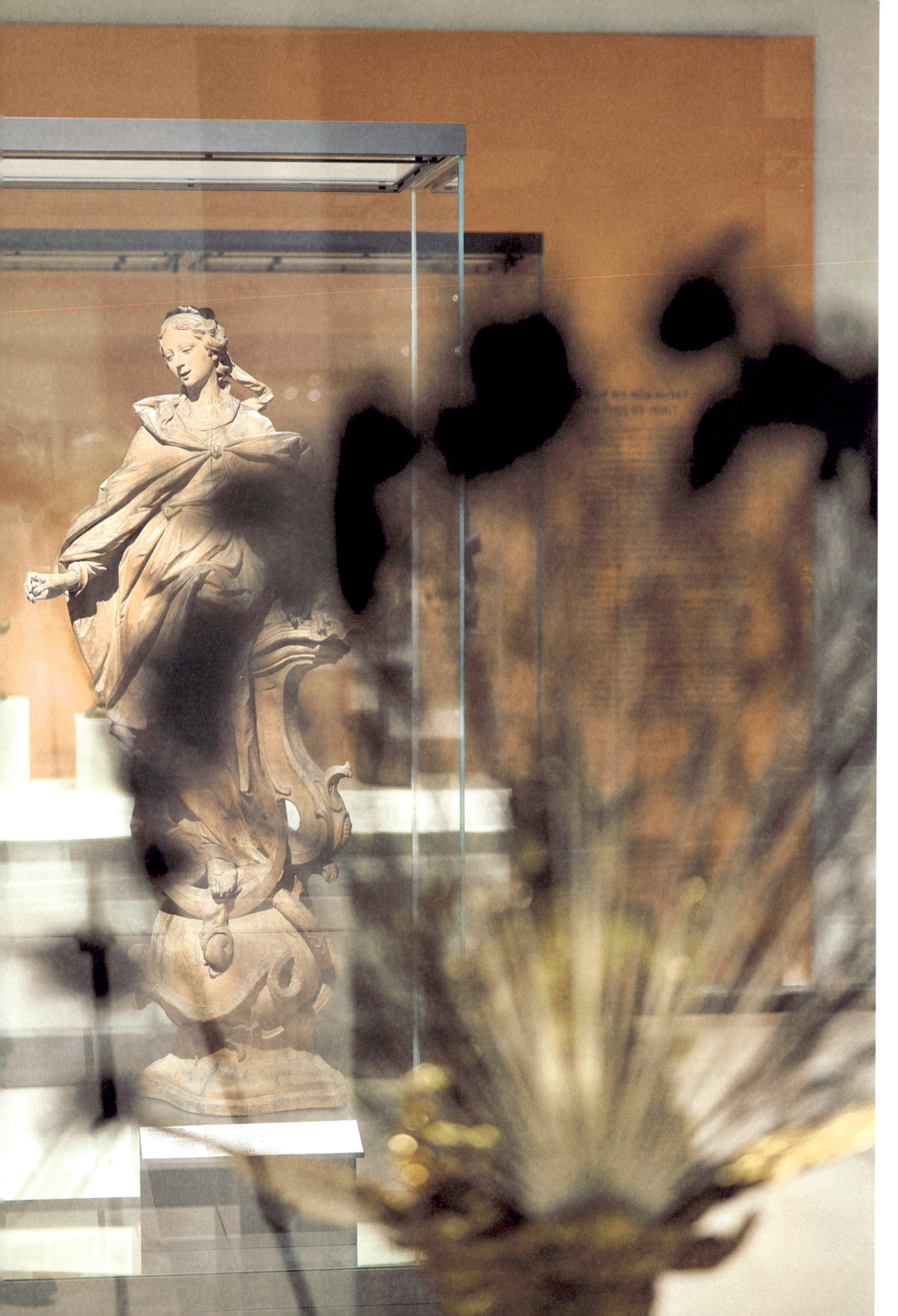

WHAT IS PROVENANCE? On the Origin of the Exhibited Objects

Provenance research in the context of museum collections entails inquiring into each object's origin from its creation up to its current whereabouts. It sets out to ascertain how objects were appropriated and the paths by which they ended up in the museum. By providing detailed information on provenance, we hope to make these paths as transparent as possible and to share the latest research findings with you. Ideally, an object's provenance will take the form of a gap-free, chronological list of its previous owners and/or custodians. The following definitions are intended to help shed light on the provenance information provided. ⸺

The author or authors of a work are always named, if known. In all other cases the label will say 'Author' or 'Authors not documented'. We would like to stress that every object was made by a skilled artisan or artist or workshop, even if their names are now lost to us or can no longer be ascertained. There may be many reasons for this. Sometimes the name of the artist or artisan was never recorded, or it was never disclosed. Often their identity was of no concern to the people who appropriated the objects, or the source materials were simply lost at some point. ⸺

But nor are the 'users or custodians' of the objects known by name in most cases. Only those who are known are included in the provenance, where they are listed chronologically up to the time the object was taken into the museum. If an object has been in the same collection for decades, the museum's historical name is mentioned alongside the one by which it is now known. ⸺

The exact circumstances under which an object was appropriated or acquired by a European user or custodian can rarely be reconstructed. The said 'collectors' were often colonial players, who might have been part of quasi-military, scientific expeditions or active as missionaries. Sometimes they quite explicitly procured objects to order for European museums. We regard colonialism as a context of systemic injustice. ⸺

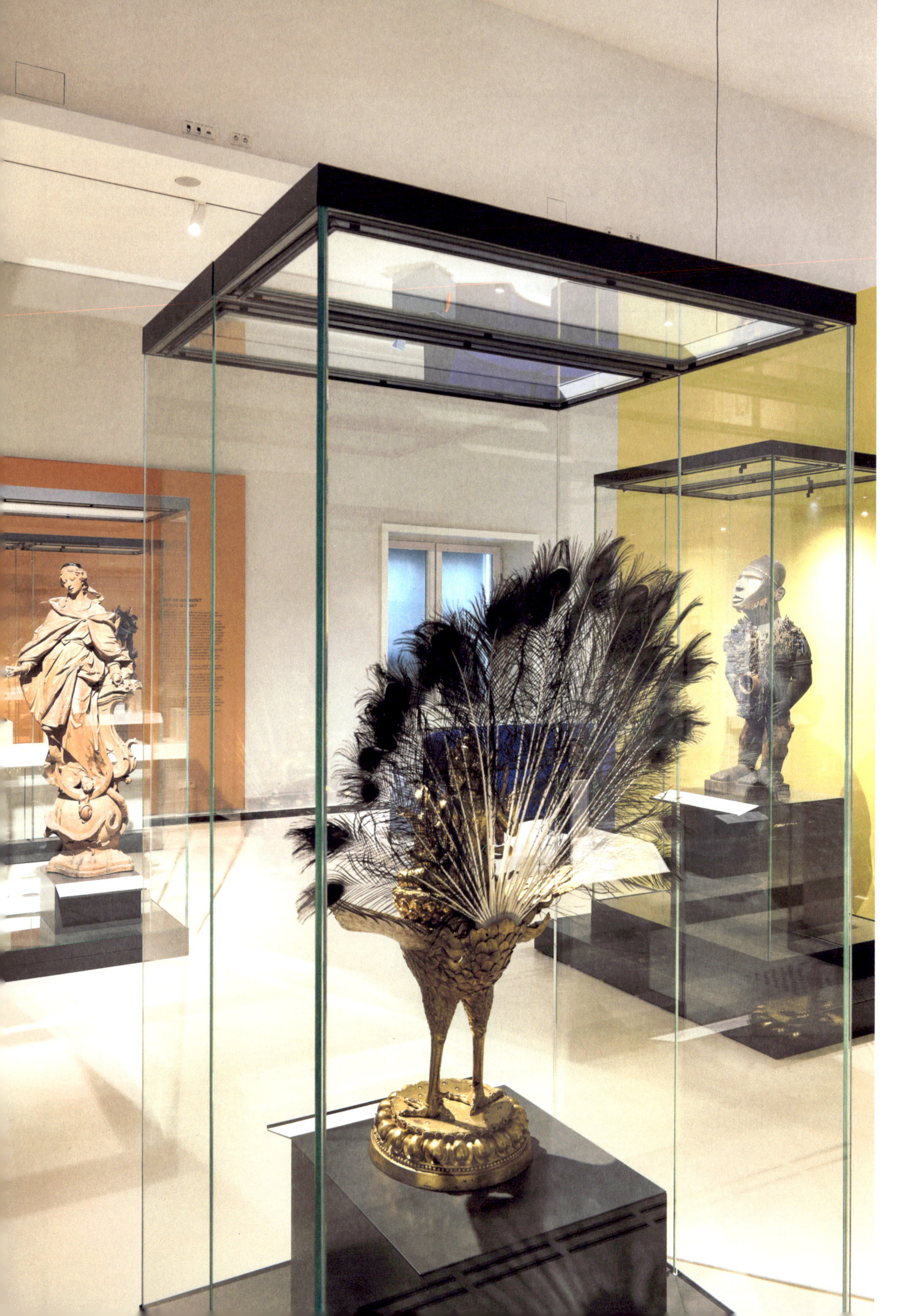

CHAPTER 1

WHAT DOES PROTECTION MEAN HERE?

The focus here is on three works whose interpretation relates to the theme of protection. They differ as much in their formal design as in the social, religious and political roles they originally played in their respective contexts. They have in common the expectation that they would mediate between this world and another, invisible world beyond. ───

Their power to protect or preserve could extend as much to individuals as to whole societies. The figures of the *VIRGIN MARY* and *MAHAMAYURI* were believed to have the ability to avert disasters such as disease, drought, famine and war. The *MANGAAKA*, by contrast, was invoked to restore social and political stability to rival Yombe communities following the collapse of the Kingdom of Loango (now part of the Republic of Congo) in 1870, in part owing to the encroaching European colonial powers. ───

Museum presentations of these objects tend not to reflect the complexity of the rituals in which they were originally embedded. They would certainly have appealed to several senses at once and through the use of potent substances, prayers, meditation or performative acts might even have been brought to life, becoming active players. In museums, by contrast, they are shown as mute, stand-alone works of art or simply as testimony to a certain society. |TS, BB| ───

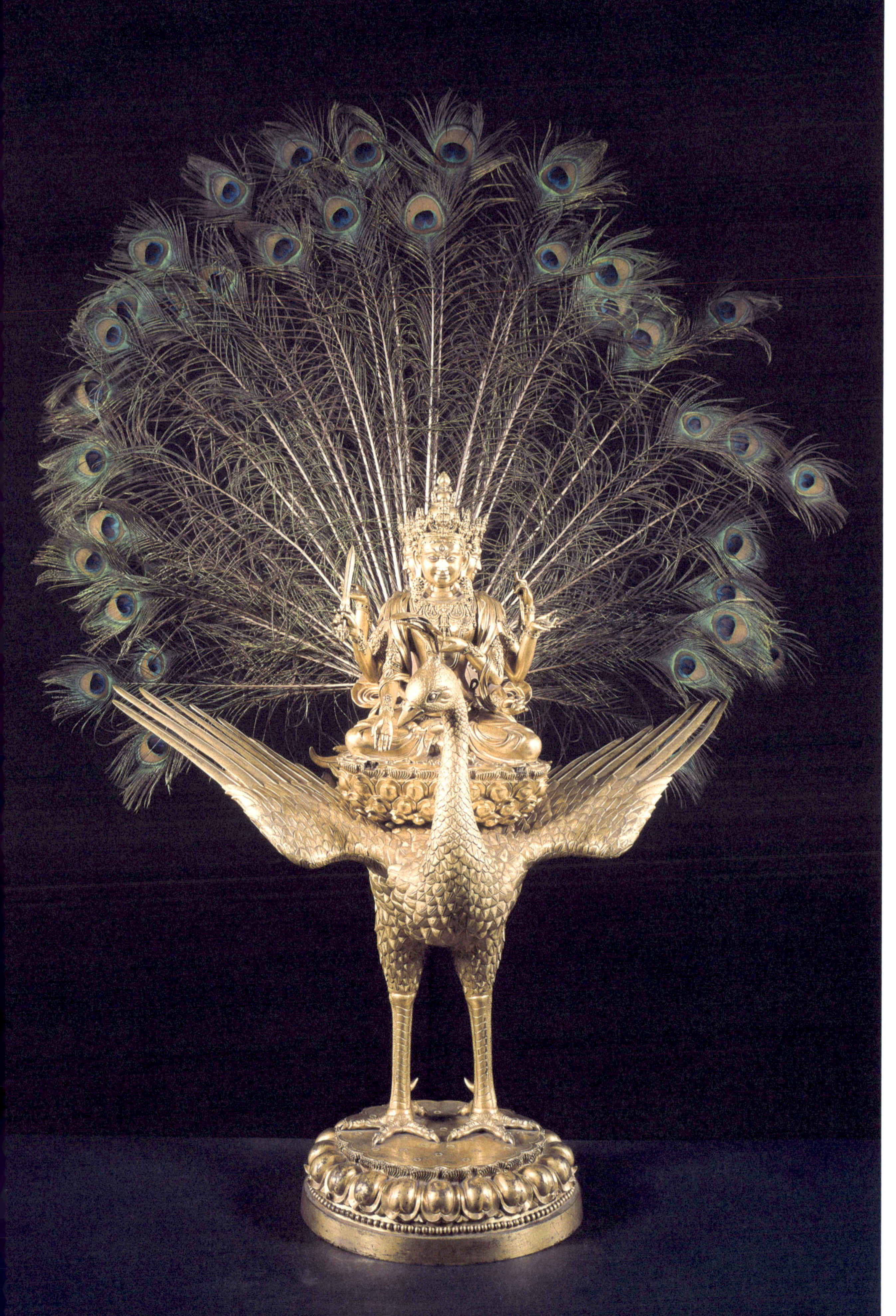

MAHAMAYURI VIDYARAJNI

Imperial workshop • Beijing (China) • Inscription dating to the Ming Xuande period (1426–1435) • fire-gilt bronze, peacock feathers • 95 × 84.5 × 47 cm (without feathers)

First known previous owner: Kunst- und Verlagshandel Rex & Co. in Berlin • Sold in 1912 to the Königliches Museum für Völkerkunde, Berlin (today: Staatliche Museen zu Berlin, Ethnologisches Museum, inv. no. I D 31831) • The object originates from a region that was partly under the influence of colonial powers from 1842 onwards. The possibility of unlawful acquisition cannot, therefore, be ruled out if it was put on the market after 1842.

The Buddhist tutelary goddess has three faces and eight arms and sits on a peacock. Of the powerful attributes that she once held in her hands, only the sword, a pot full of jewels, and the shaft of a banner of victory have been preserved. This representation of the *MAHAMAYURI VIDYARAJNI* ('great peacock queen of wisdom') symbolises the power of the fearless peacock that eats even venomous snakes. She arose in India as the embodiment of protection against snakebite and disease. In eighth-century China, by contrast, the four-armed deity became the centrepiece of an imperial ritual, whose purpose was to keep the rain-giving dragon in check and so ensure a bountiful harvest and with it the stability of the whole empire. The figure is therefore important to the history of culture in that it attests to complex, inner-Asian crosscurrents. The eight-armed version of the peacock goddess is an amalgam of two different Buddhist concepts of Mahamayuri that developed independently of each other in time and place. The figure was created in the early fifteenth century at the court of the Ming Dynasty under the influence of Tibetan monks and Nepalese artists. |BB|

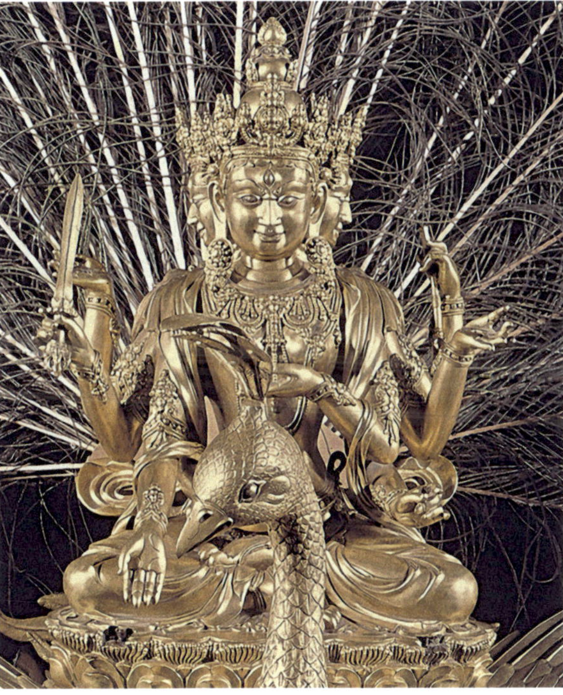

Detail of the Buddhist tutelary deity *Mahamayuri Vidyarajni*

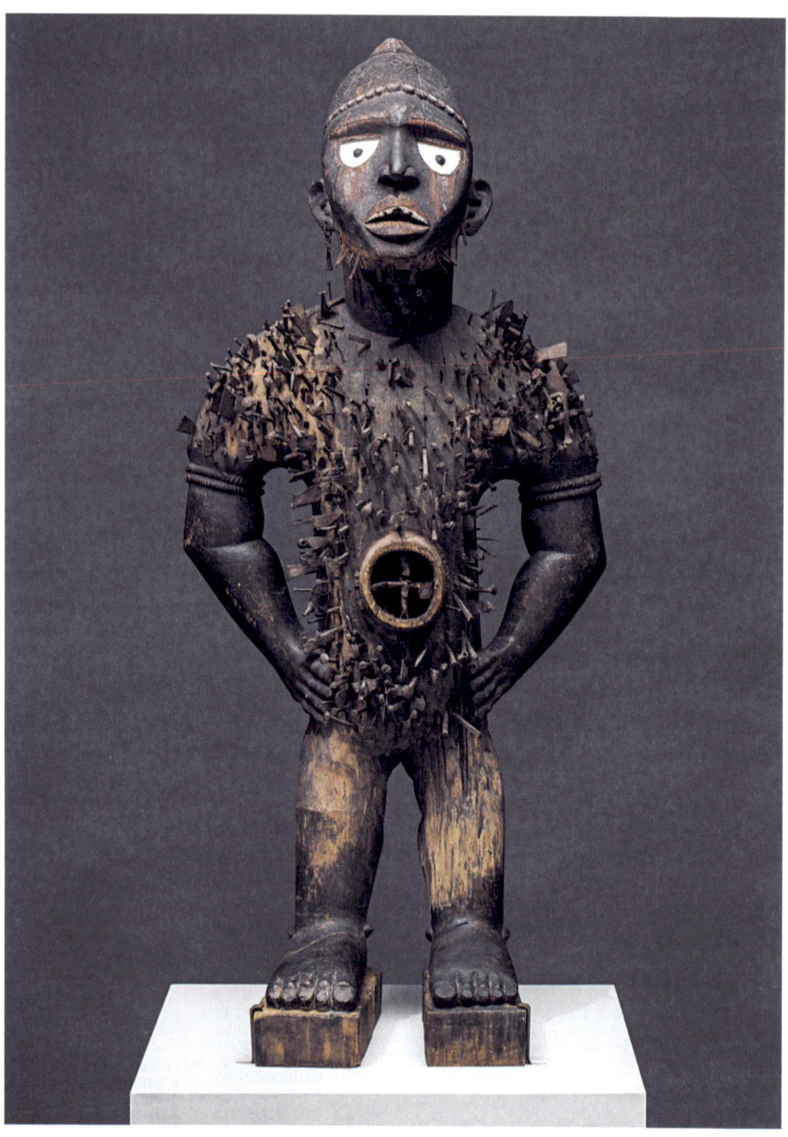

MANGAAKA
(NKISI NKONDI)

Authors not documented • Yombe region on the river Chiloango (DR Congo, Republic of Congo, or Cabinda, Angola) • second half of 19th cent. • wood, iron, porcelain, pigments • 120 × 54 × 38.5 cm

Users, custodians before European appropriation not documented • Robert Visser, from 1882–1904 plantation manager in "Congo Free State", "French Congo" and "Portuguese Congo" • Gifted in 1904 to the Königliches Museum für Völkerkunde, Berlin (today: Staatliche Museen zu Berlin, Ethnologisches Museum, inv. no. III C 17114) • The object originates from a region that was under colonial rule at the time of its appropriation. We regard colonialism as a context of systemic injustice. Thus even gifts and documented purchases cannot invariably be regarded as having been lawfully acquired.

The figure stands facing us in the pose of a Congolese ruler, staring at us intently with wide open eyes. The large upper body is studded with dozens of metal parts that accentuate the abdominal cavity. This would have been filled with *BILONGO*, that is, with potent substances that endowed the figure with superhuman powers. This particular type of figure, *MANGAAKA*, began appearing in 1865. It was intended as moral support that would strengthen social cohesion between the various communities in the severely destabilised Yombe region as well as keeping 'evil forces' at bay. The seventeen such *ZINKONDI* (sing. *NKONDI*) that still exist in various Western collections were probably made by the same few workshops. |TS|

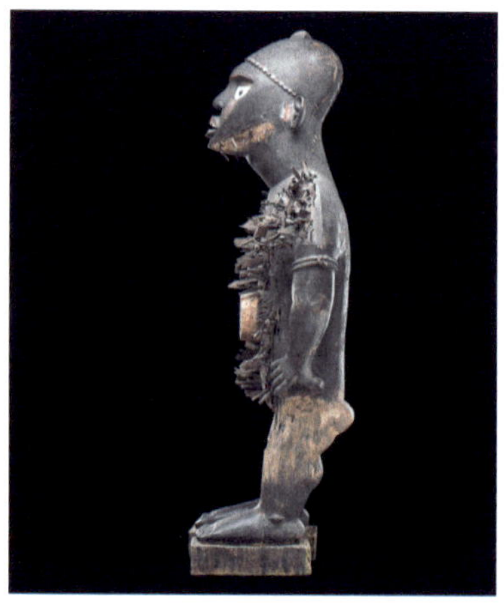

MARY STANDING ON THE EARTH (IMMA-CULATA CONCEPTIO)

Author not documented • Parish church of Gerolsheim (Germany) • Mid-18th century • limewood • 164 × 72 × 39 cm

First known previous owner: Georg Schuster, in the first half of 20th cent. sculptor and woodwork restorer in Munich • Sold in 1908 to the Kaiser-Friedrich-Museum, Berlin (today: Staatliche Museen zu Berlin, Skulpturensammlung und Museum für Byzantinische Kunst, inv. no. 5561) • No evidence of unjust acquisition is known of at this time.

This depiction of the ***VIRGIN MARY*** as a young girl wearing her hair loose is intended to express the Immaculate Conception. Clad in long, flowing robes, Mary stands triumphantly on top of the earth complete with crescent moon. She would originally have held a lily sceptre symbolising her purity. Her left foot is crushing the snake coiled around the moon and globe. The serpent represents the Fall, the Devil, and evil in Christian iconography. In 1439, the Council of Basel declared Mary to be untouched by original sin. According to Christian theology, it was the disobedience of Adam and Eve that led to the breach with God. Only through the incarnation, death and resurrection of Jesus Christ as the Son of God could their descendants hope for forgiveness and reconciliation with God. Up until the Reformation, the Mother of God was regarded throughout Christendom as humanity's most important intercessor and a source of solace and hope and is still so regarded in the Catholic Church. She is also the patron saint of Bavaria, where this sculpture was made. |HUK|

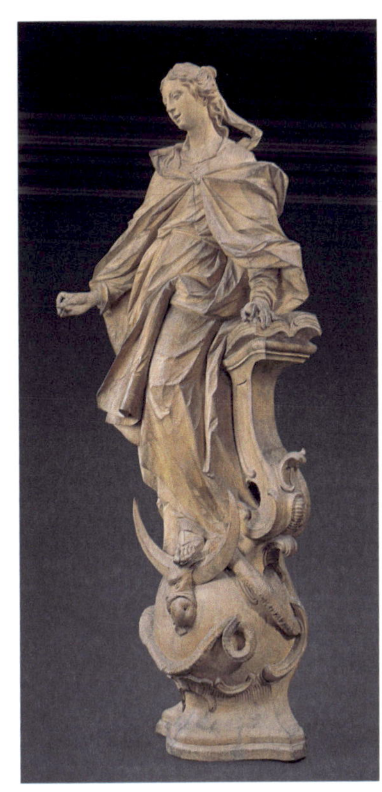

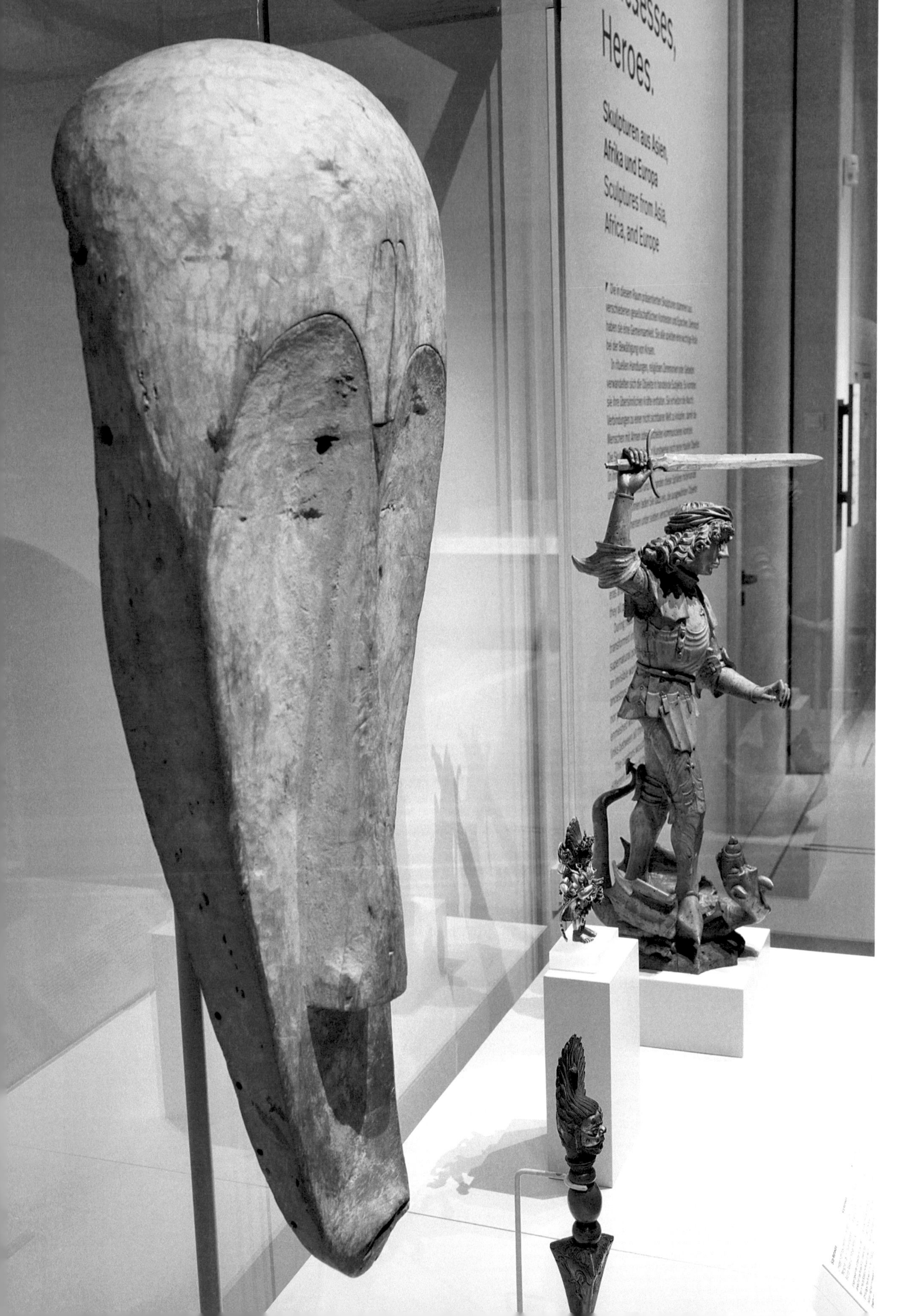
…cesses,
Heroes.
Skulpturen aus Asien,
Afrika und Europa
Sculptures from Asia,
Africa, and Europe

CHAPTER 2

HOW TO KEEP EVIL FORCES IN CHECK?

The works shown in this chapter were all born of the need to keep fears or destructive forces at bay: the mask reminiscent of a skull, the raised sword, the stake for pinning down demons and the wrathful face all speak a seemingly unambiguous language. Yet the precise meaning of these objects was always malleable, never static or set in stone, and at various times it was adapted in line with changed circumstances or even redefined altogether. ⸻

We know that Central European depictions of Saint George, like the one shown here, were intended to give courage and hope to the devout in times of peril. By contrast, we know little about the mask from Central Africa. According to one interpretation, it served as a warning of death to anyone who dared transgress against the prevailing social norms. ⸻

All four objects played a part in individual or collective rituals and only in such a ritual context did they unfold their true potency. Their impressive visuals, moreover, would have been legible to members of the society that produced them, but not necessarily to outsiders. ⸻

The museum presentation highlights the variety of visual forms of expression, proving that there are no limits to human inventiveness and creativity, even in works prompted by the same concerns. The designs differ greatly because each of them was shaped by a specific conceptual world. |BL, TS| ⸻

NGIL MASK

Authors not documented •
Fang Region (Gabon
or Cameroon) • 19th cent. •
wood, lime paint •
75 × 29 × 19 cm

Users, custodians before
European appropriation not
documented • H. Oelert •
Sold in 1895 to the Königliches Museum für Völker-
kunde, Berlin (today: Staatliche Museen zu Berlin,
Ethnologisches Museum, inv.
no. III C 6000) • The object
originates from a region
that was under colonial rule
at the time of its appro-
priation. We regard colonialism as a context of systemic.
Thus even gifts and docu-
mented purchases cannot
invariably be regarded
as having been lawfully acquired.

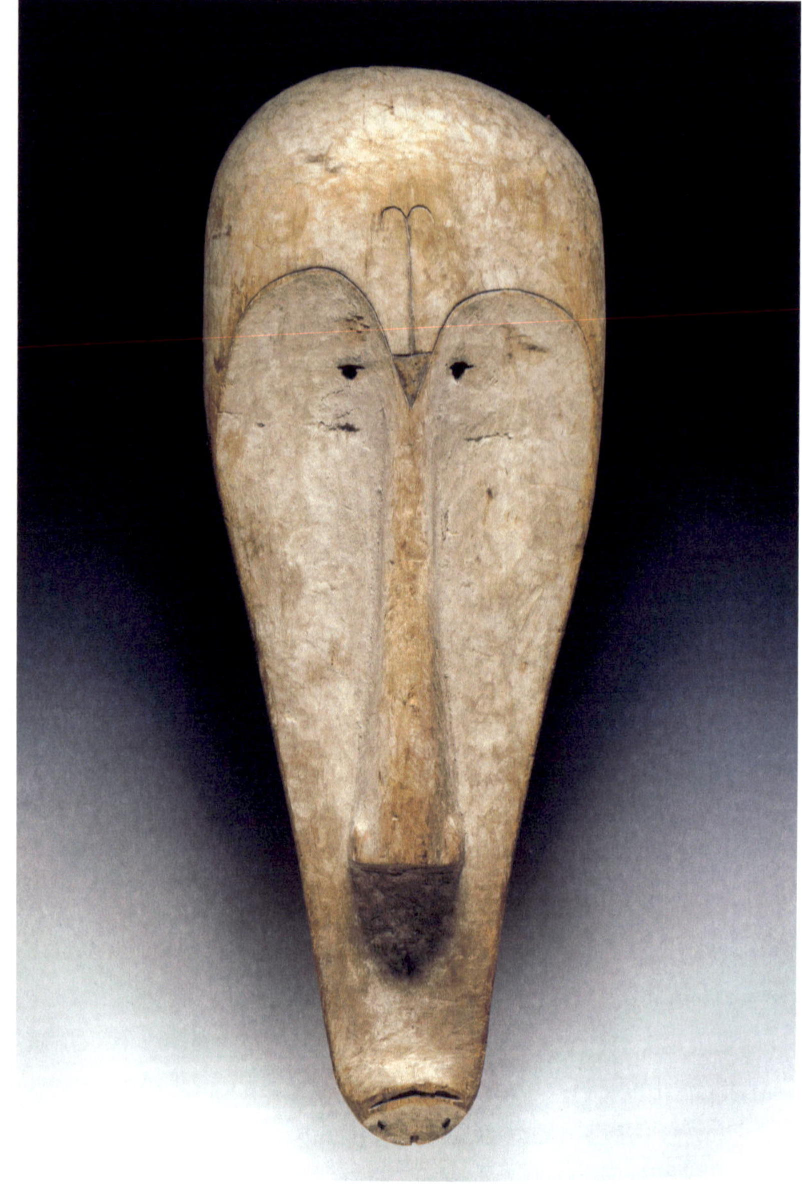

The mask was crucial to the complex dispensation of justice
by the *NGIL*, a secret society of the Fang in Central Africa. As
the relevant publications on the art of Gabon explain, the
mask performed various functions. It was believed to offer protection from poisoning, repel dangerous forces, and unmask
and punish evildoers. As it stood for the imminent jurisdiction
of the Ngil, its appearance typically instilled fear into members of the Fang.[1] The mask's white face symbolises the
presence of ancestors and spirits. It serves as a reminder that
transgressions will be punished by death or banishment.[2] In
the belief system of the Fang, the authority of the Ngil visual-
ised by the mask was a powerful inducement to abide by the
prevailing social norms. The French colonial government out-
lawed Ngil rituals in 1910.[3] |TS|

RITUAL DAGGER (SANSKRIT: KILA)

Author not documented • Tibet (China) or Mongolia • 19th cent. • copper, parcel-gilt • 32 × 9 × 5.5 cm

First known previous owner: Dr. Adam • Sold in 1912 to the Königliches Museum für Völkerkunde, Berlin (today: Staatliche Museen zu Berlin, Ethnologisches Museum, inv. no. I D 31974) • No evidence of unjust acquisition is known of at this time.

This stake-like ritual dagger is for conquering negative forces, subjugating demons and eradicating all obstacles on the path to enlightenment.[5] The pommel is shaped like the head of the tutelary god Hayagriva, a wrathful embodiment of the empathetic *BODHISATTVA AVALOKITESHVARA* |see p. 83|. His attribute is the tiny horse's head nestling in his shaggy hair. The haft culminates in a three-sided point, which was ritually thrust into the heart of the demon to symbolically pin down the forces of evil – when building a house, say. This ritual is still practised today |see below|. |BB|

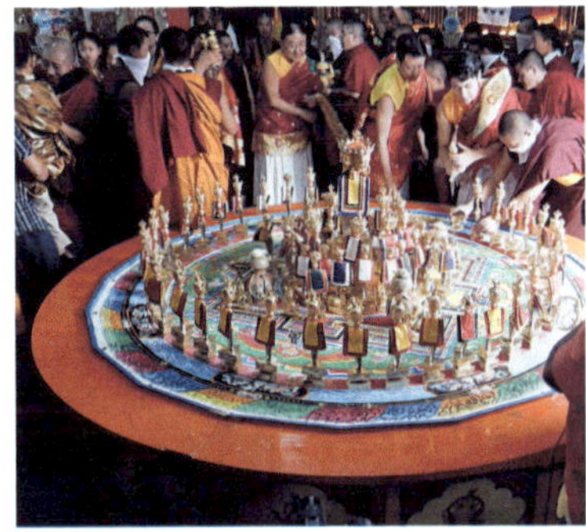

Vajrakila ritual with the Supreme Master of the Sakya School of Buddhism in Tibet, the 41st Sakya Trizin Ngawang Kunga Thegchen Pelbar, Rajpur, India

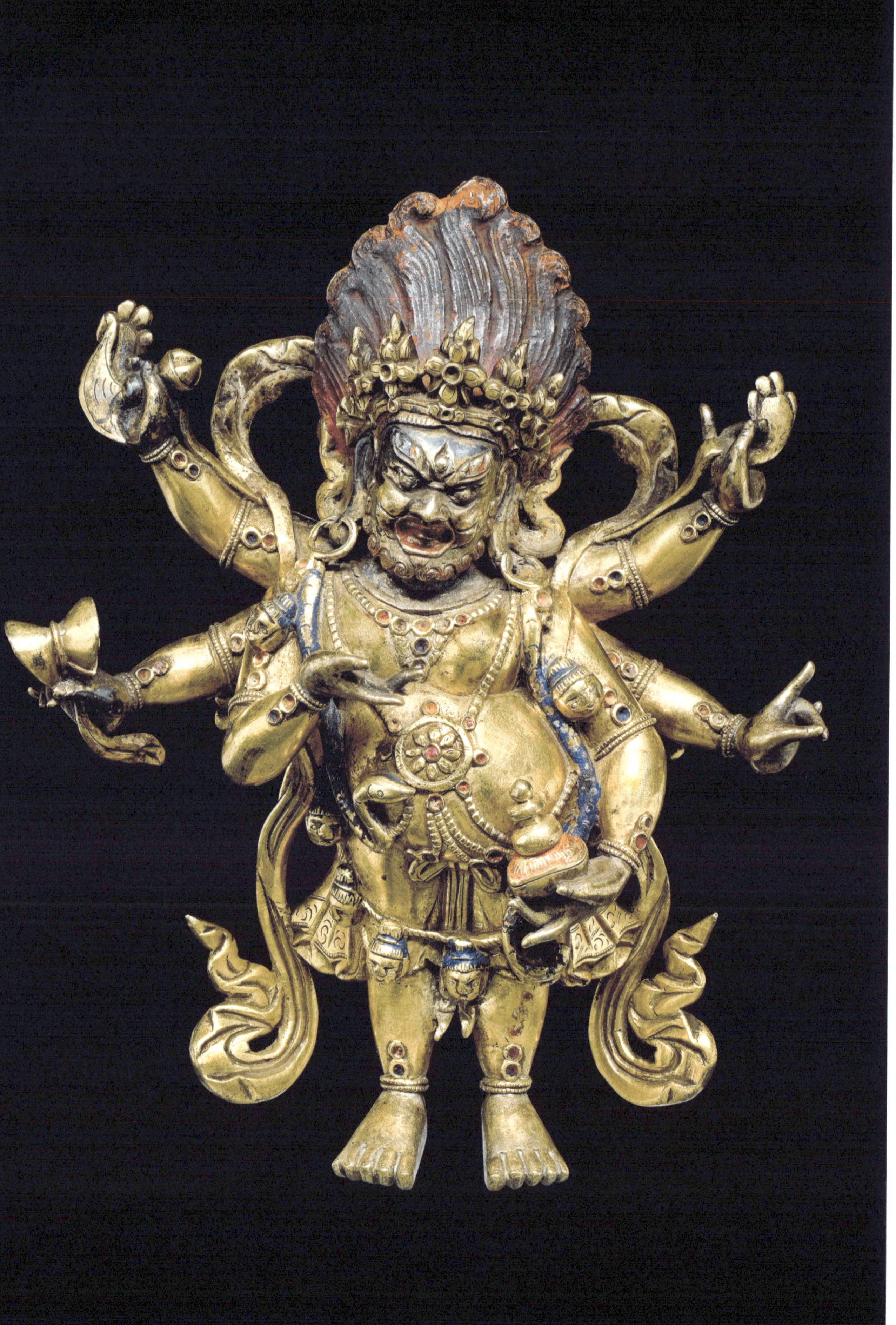

SITA MAHAKALA

Author not documented •
Ulan Bator (Mongolia) •
18th cent. • Fire-gilt bronze,
traces of polychromy •
15 × 12.7 × 5.5 cm

First known previous owner:
Mr. Lau • Sold in 1967 to
the Museum für Völkerkunde,
Berlin (today: Staatliche
Museen zu Berlin, Ethnologisches Museum, inv. no.
I D 46202) • No evidence of
unjust acquisition is known
of at this time.

In Tibetan Buddhism Mahakalas are tutelary gods who keep inner and outer demons at bay. They do this by assuming the demons' own terrifying appearance. The six-armed, *SITA MAHAKALA* is responsible for battling the inner demons to ensure that the monastery prospers.[4] So furious is he that his hair is standing on end, his three eyes are bulging, and his wide-open mouth is bristling with fangs. He wears an ele-phant-skin cloak, a garland of severed heads, bone jewellery and a snake. In his hands, he holds a chopper, a drum made of skulls and a bowl with a treasure vase. What are missing, along with the wish-fulfilling jewel in the right hand pressed to his breast, are the two elephant-headed Ganesh figures on which he originally stood |see below|, the whereabouts of which are unknown. |BB|

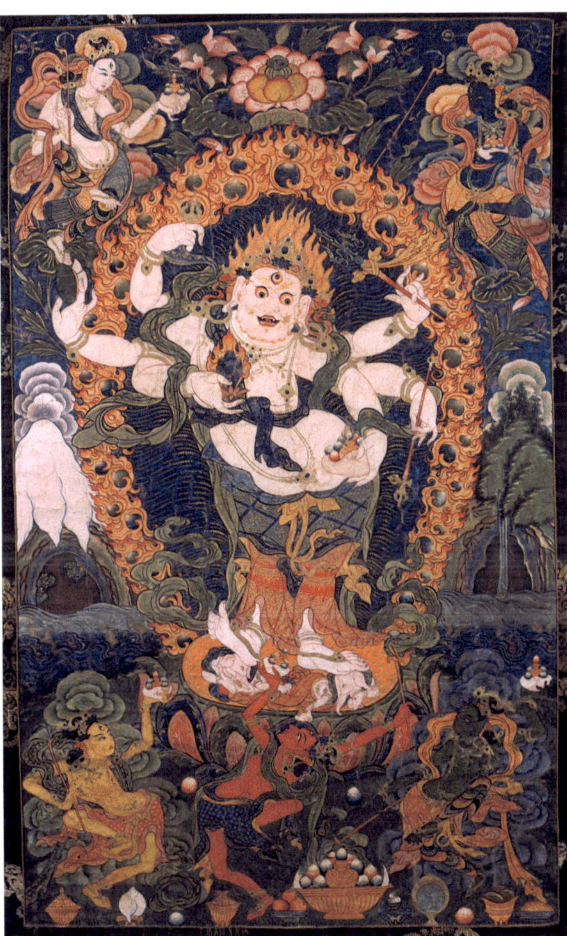

The White Maha-kala, Shadbhuja, Tibet, 18th century, pigments on cloth

Rubin Museum of Art, Gift of Shelley and Donald Rubin, C2006.66.28 (HAR 813)

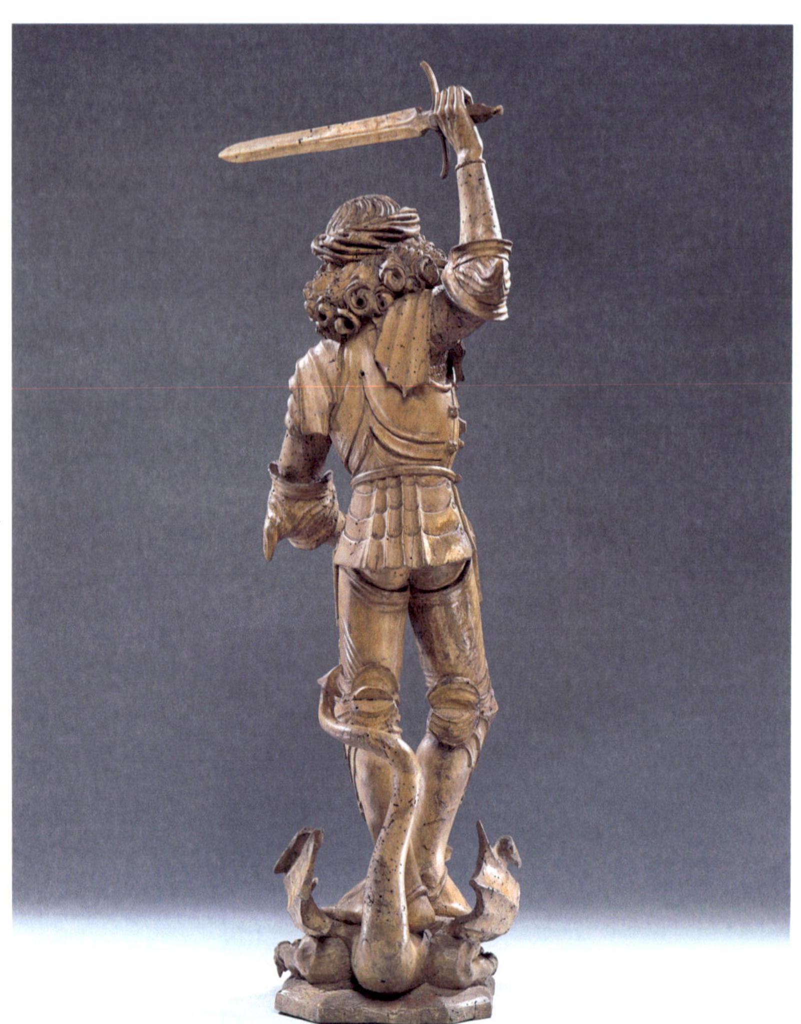

SAINT GEORGE

Author not documented •
Tyrol (Austria) • c. 1490 •
limewood • 76 × 40 × 28 cm

First known previous owner:
James Simon, c. 1900
entrepreneur and patron of
the arts in Berlin • Gifted
in 1918 to the Kaiser-Friedrich-Museum, Berlin (today:
Staatliche Museen zu Berlin,
Skulpturensammlung und
Museum für Byzantinische
Kunst, inv. no. 8179) • No
evidence of unjust acquisition is known of at this time.

Legends tell of a Roman soldier called George who saved a princess from being sacrificed to a dragon. This sculpture shows him wearing the armour of a medieval knight and brandishing the sword with which he will slay the dragon sprawled on the ground. Despite the high drama of the scene, the sculpture is remarkably passive. Assured of eventual victory, the saint stands with both feet firmly planted on the writhing, but no longer threatening monster. The style of the piece leaves us in no doubt as to the eventual outcome of the duel.

In Christian iconography, images of Saint George, whether with or without the princess, symbolise the battle between good and evil.[6] The artist of this piece persuades us that the Christian knight, armed with his faith, can be sure of triumphing over evil, be it in the form of heresy or a natural calamity. The sculpture was probably set up on an altar in a church, where it would have served both as a role model of the virtuous life and as a source of hope and courage for the anxious devout. |JC|

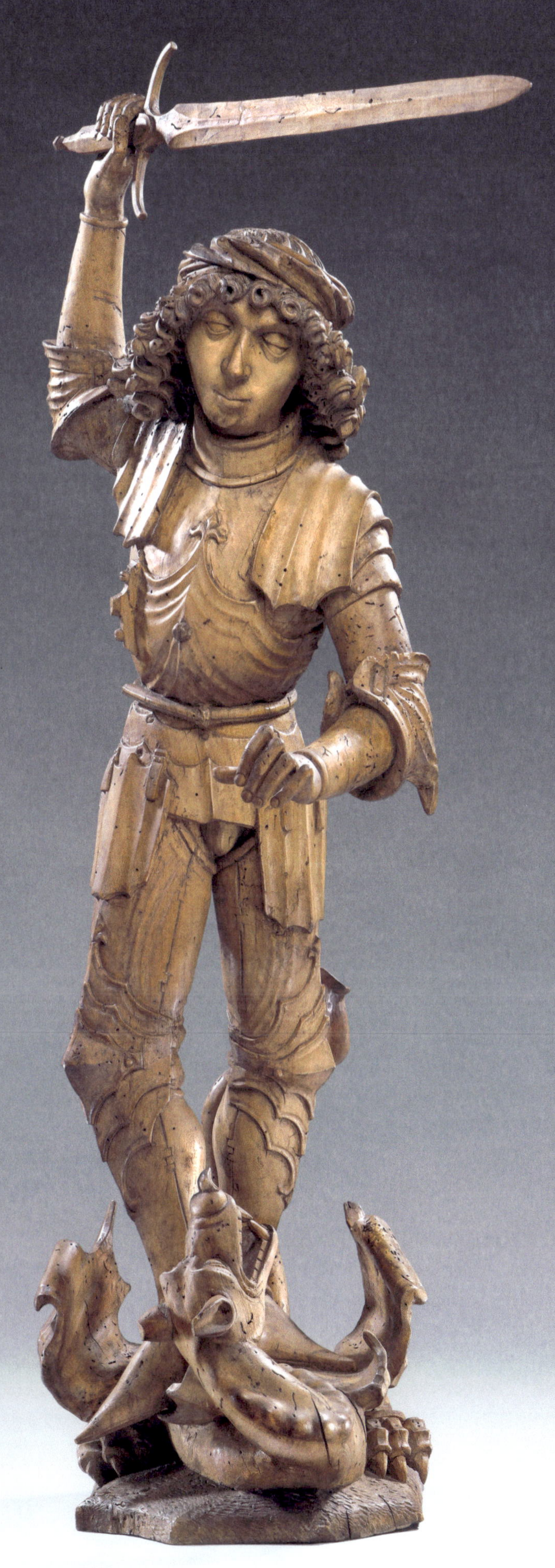

7

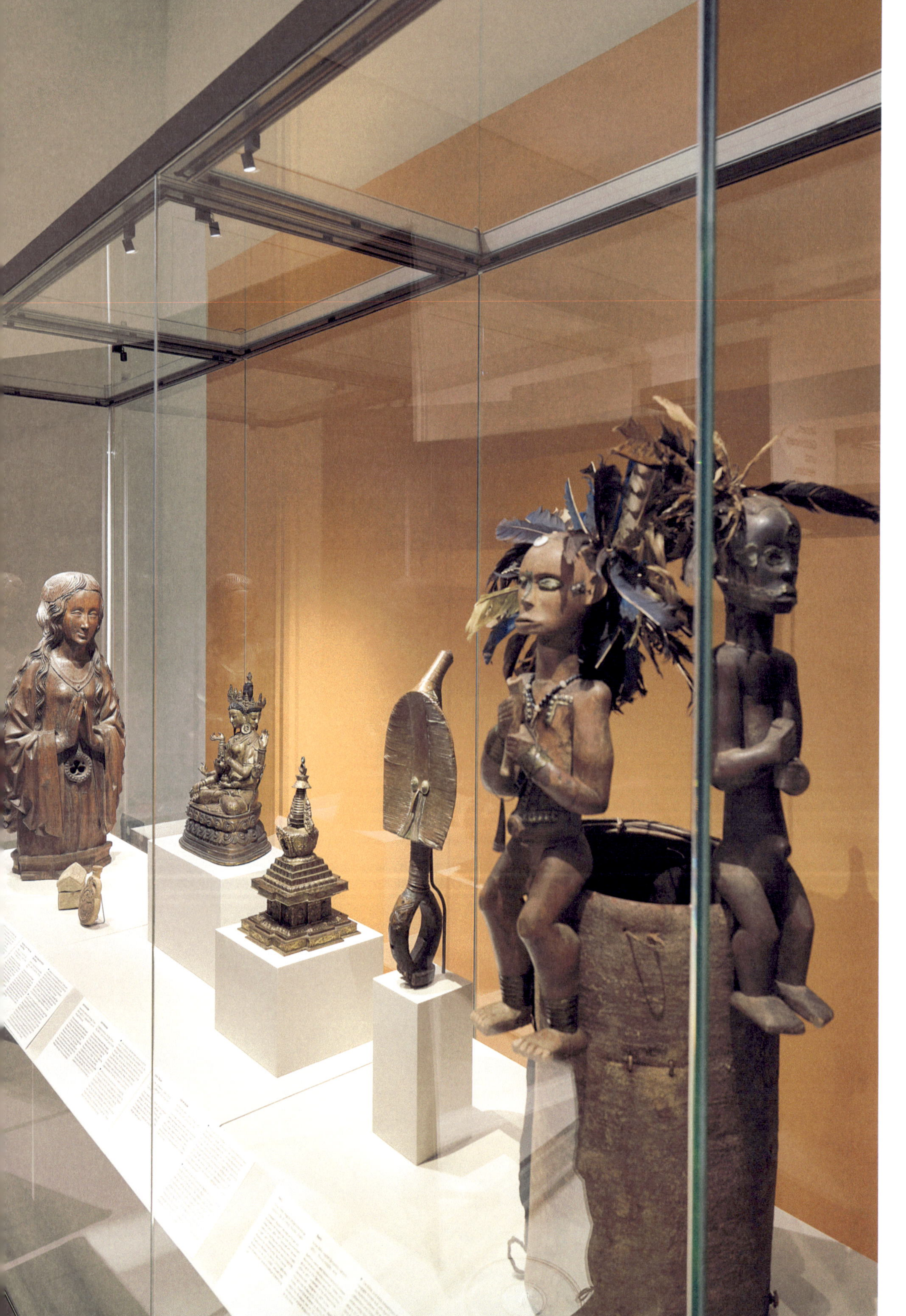

ARE THEY ALL REAL?

Every object in this chapter was created as a receptacle (or part thereof) for materials that forged a link to a particular person or group. Western museums tend to classify all such objects as reliquaries, despite their very different functional contexts. In the Christian faith, 'relics' (Latin for 'left behind') are either the mortal remains of an individual (Jesus Christ, the Virgin Mary, or a saint) or an object touched by the said person, which have since become an object of veneration. That the relic is genuine is obviously of the utmost importance in such a context. In Buddhism it is the ashes of the Buddha or one of his worthy successors that are worshipped, though objects and doctrinal texts might also be selected and declared sacred by a person of exceptional 'spirituality'. Many Central African belief systems hold the skull to be the seat of a person's vital powers. Accordingly, it was the skulls of highly esteemed ancestors that were preserved and worshipped there.[1] Relics make the presence of the deceased palpable. As we are dealing here with human remains, the presentation of these objects in museums is highly controversial. |JC| —

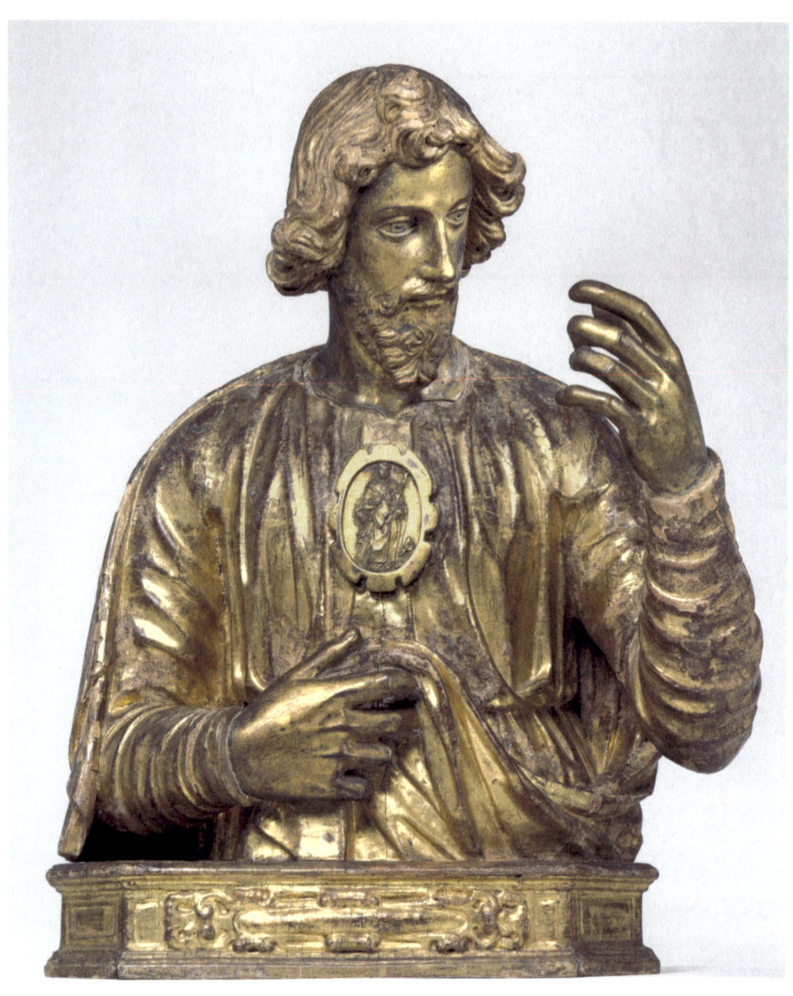

RELIQUARY BUST OF A SAINT

Author not documented (Spain) • 2nd half of 16th cent. • wood, metal, polychromy and gilding • 65.5 × 53.5 × 42.8 cm

Possible previous owners not documented • Peter Mavrogordato, archaeologist, from 1916 advisor to the Königliche Museen in Berlin • Sold in 1980 from Mavrogordato's estate to the Staatliche Museen zu Berlin, Skulpturensammlung, inv. no. 8743 • No evidence of unjust acquisition is known of at this time.

The relics inside this bust are probably those of Saint Dominic or a member of his order. They are completely hidden from view, the only visible pointer to them being the seal-like medallion |see right|. This shows Dominic with his attributes: a crucifix, a star and a dog carrying a flaming torch in its mouth (which is an allusion to the vision that Dominic's mother had shortly before his birth, in which a dog sprang out of her womb and set the earth ablaze).[2] The brooch recalls a wax seal like those appended to glass reliquaries or the cloth wrappings of reliquary bundles. It can therefore be read, at least by implication, as a seal of quality and authenticity for the relics inside the figure, even as it renders them inaccessible. |AS|

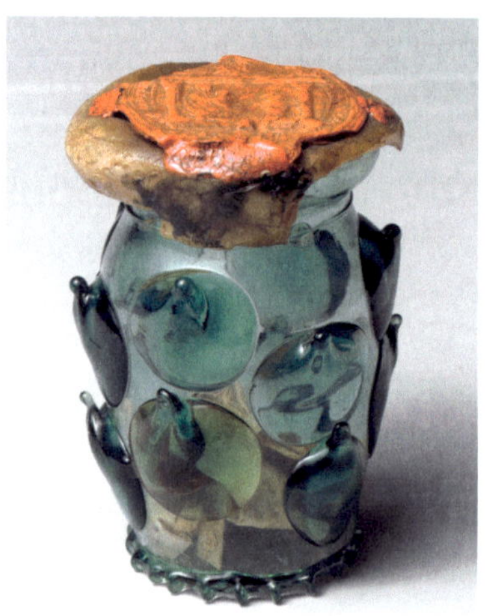

Glass reliquary (Germany), late 15th century, glass, wax, silk, linen, ink on parchment, 10.3 × 7.5 cm
The Metropolitan Museum of Art, New York, The Cloisters Collection

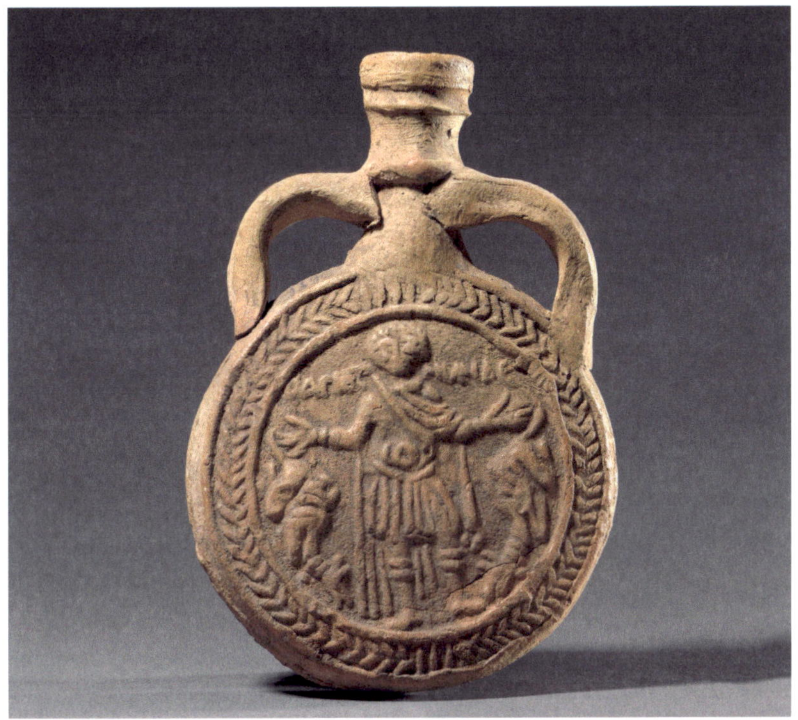

9

Abu Mina, c. 45 kilometres south-west of Alexandria, was one of the most important Christian shrines of Late Antiquity. It owes its name to Saint Menas, an Egyptian soldier who according to legend was martyred in Phrygia (now in Turkey) during the persecution of the Christians under Emperor Diocletian.[3] Menas's body was sent back to Egypt by ship and then taken into the desert by caravan. After stopping for a rest, the camels refused to continue their journey, which was read as a sign that Menas's resting place had been reached. The burial site of Abu Mina became a place of veneration and until its destruction during the Persian occupation (619–629) attracted countless pilgrims from all over the Roman Empire. Pilgrim's flasks like this one, also called ampullae, were sold as souvenirs at the shrine. They could be filled with water, oil or sand taken from the ground near the grave. The pilgrims hoped that this would assure them of the saint's protection on their homeward journey.[4] |CF|

PILGRIM'S FLASK WITH MOTIF OF SAINT MENAS

Author not documented • Alexandria (Egypt) • Late 5th–mid-7th cent. • pottery, fired • 15 × 10 cm (diameter of the body)

First known previous owner: Eduard Friedheim, in the second half of 19th cent. attorney and collector in Alexandria • Purchased in 1900–01 by Josef Strzygowski, art historian and from 1892–1909 Professor of Art History at the University of Graz, on behalf of the Kaiser-Friedrich-Museum, Berlin (today: Staatliche Museen zu Berlin, Skulpturensammlung und Museum für Byzantinische Kunst, inv. no. 3396) • No evidence of unjust acquisition is known of at this time.

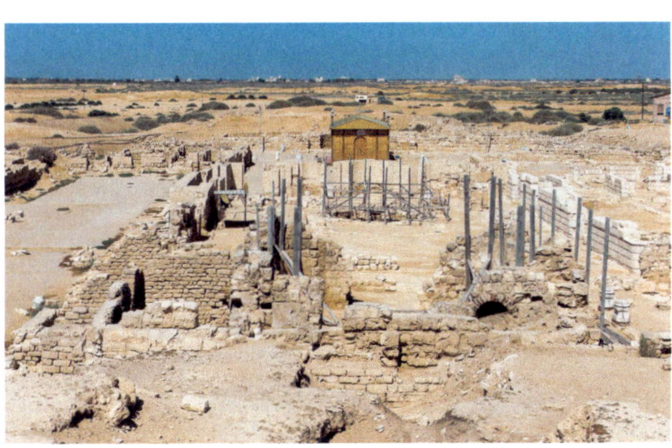

Religious complex at Abu Mena (XIII). A view of the cluster of structures at the eastern end of the Great Basilica, photograph from 2013

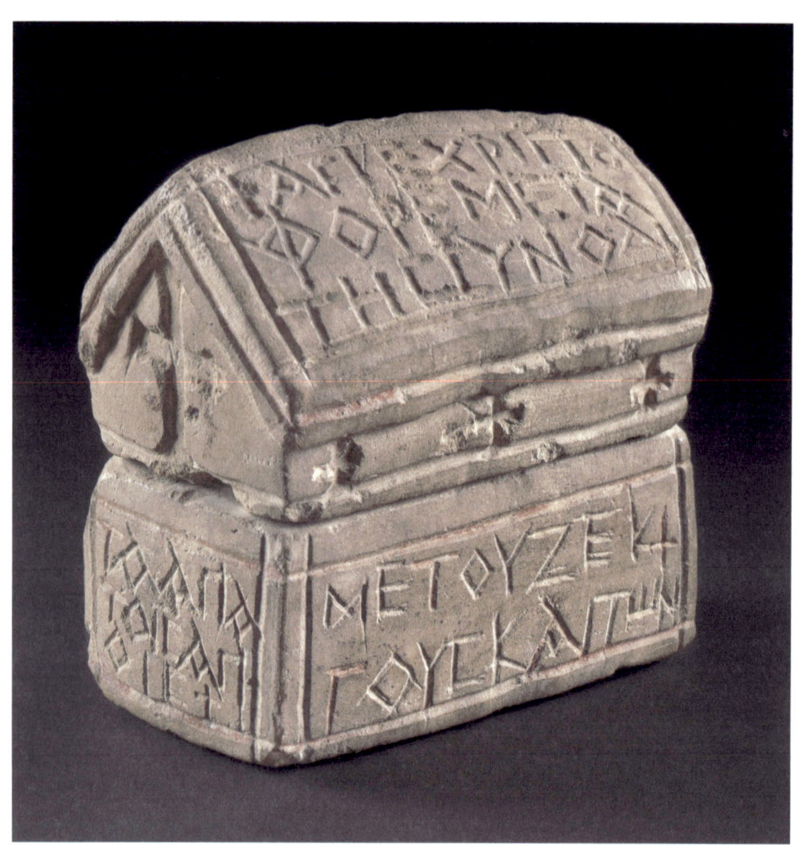

RELIQUARY IN THE SHAPE OF A SARCOPHAGUS

Author not documented •
Constantinople (Byzantine
Empire, today: Turkey) •
5th–7th cent. • Limestone •
5.5 × 10.5 × 6.3 cm

The art market (probably) •
Purchased in 1929, possibly
through Martin Schede,
from 1910–1929 archaeolo-
gist in Turkey and agent
for the Staatliche Museen,
by the Frühchristlich-
Byzantinische Sammlung,
Berlin (today: Staatliche
Museen zu Berlin, Skulpturensammlung und Museum
für Byzantinische Kunst, inv.
no. 9517) • The object originates from a region in
which exports of archaeo-
logical artefacts were
prohibited at the time of its
sale to the Frühchristlich-
Byzantinische Sammlung.
That it was traded illegally
cannot, therefore, be
ruled out.

Shaped like a Late Antique sarcophagus with gable roof, this
stone reliquary contains relics – probably bones – of a venerated person. The Greek inscription on the roof and sides is by
a man named Elpidin, who addresses Saint Christopher di-
rectly and solicits his help for himself, his wife, and his children.
As the words appeal to the saint in person, it seems likely that
the relics inside are his.
A church dedicated to Saint Christopher in the ancient city of
Chalcedon – now Kadıköy in Istanbul – was consecrated in
the year 452,[5] and it is possible that the reliquary comes from
there. Chest-shaped reliquaries like this one generally stood
where worshippers could see them and touch them, so in the
church itself, in a side chapel, or underneath the altar. What
is unusual here is that the donor seeks succour specifically for
himself and his family, even though the protection of such rel-
ics extended to all believers. |JC|

VOTIVE STUPA

Author not documented •
Tibet (China) • 19th cent. •
parcel-gilt copper
alloy, turquoise inlay •
35 × 20 × 20 cm

First known previous owner:
Julius Konietzko, explorer
and trader • Sold in 1963 to
the Museum für Völkerkunde,
Berlin (today: Staatliche
Museen zu Berlin, Ethnologisches Museum, inv. no.
I D 37441) • No evidence of
unjust acquisition is known
of at this time.

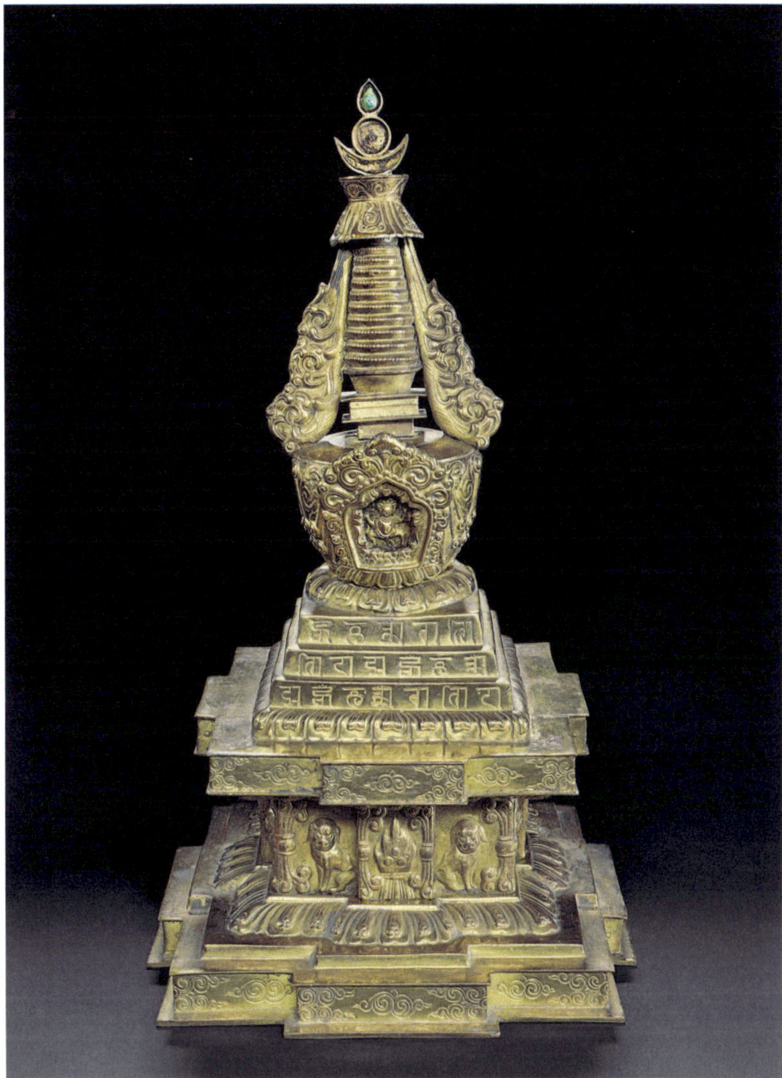

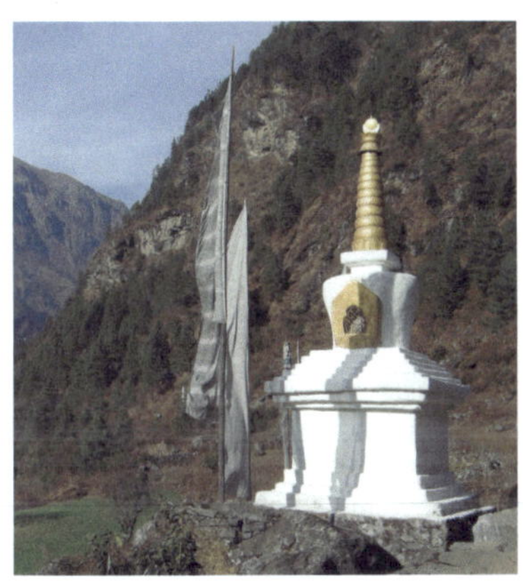

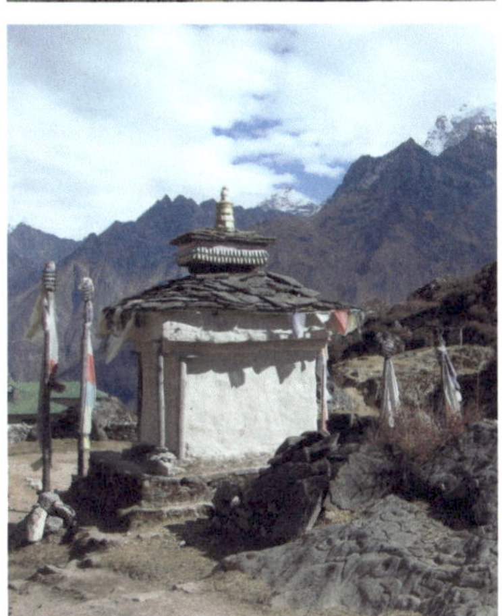

Stupa, Khumbu Himal, Nepal,
photograph from 2008

Originally conceived as a monumental burial mound and place
of remembrance, the stupa symbolizes the Buddhist cosmos.
The stepped square base represents the earth, the dome-
shaped superstructure the firmament and the canopy on the
vertical axis the cosmic spheres |see left|.[6] A votive stupa can
serve as a reliquary for the remains of a deceased Buddhist
teacher, sacred texts, cult figures, votive tablets or medicinal
herbs.[7] This makes it an object of veneration that bestows protection and blessings on the faithful. Hence the protective man-
tras engraved in Indian syllabic script on the steps below the
dome of this stupa. |BB|

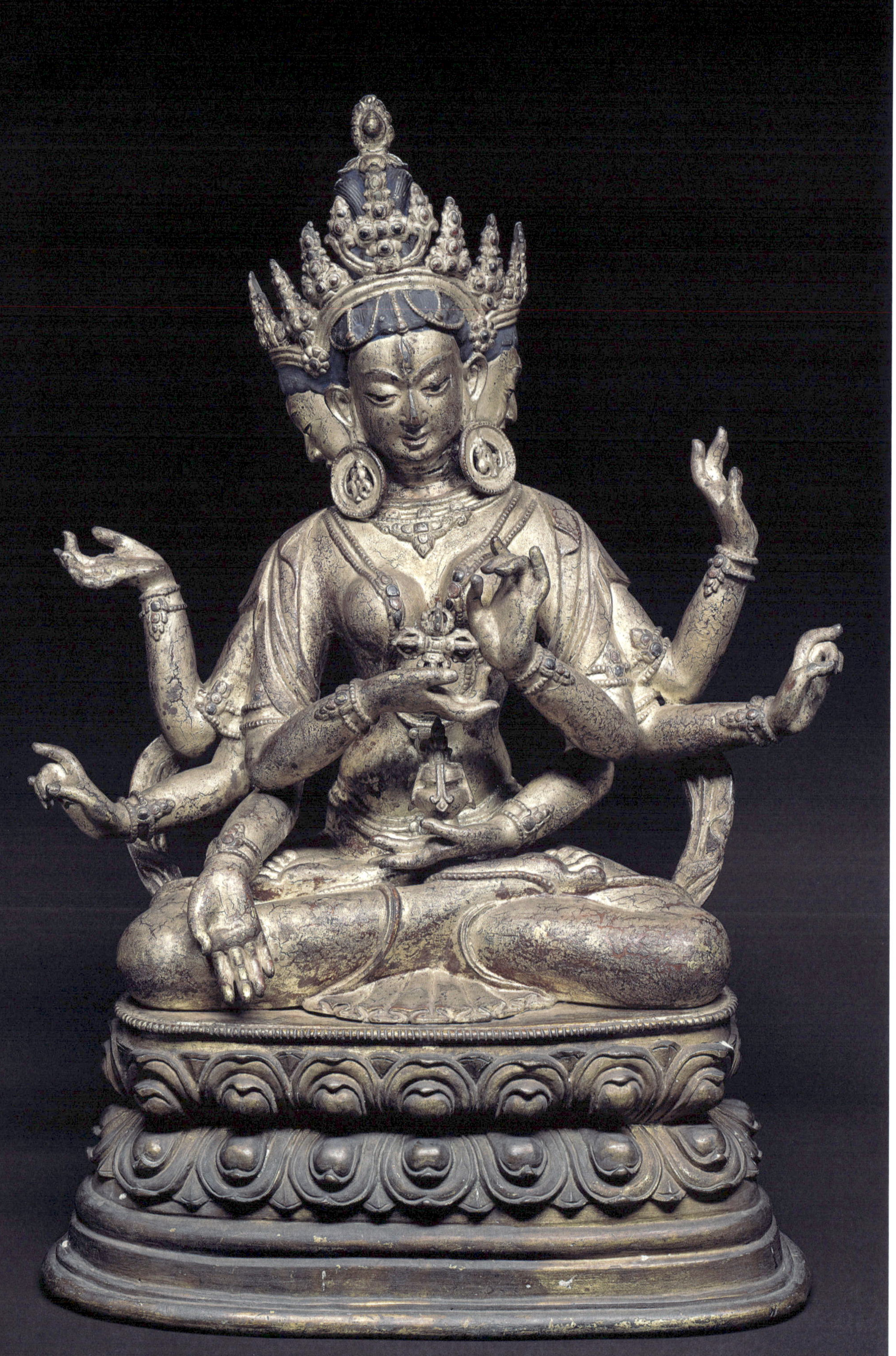

USHNISHAVIJAYA

Imperial workshop • Beijing (China) • Mid-18th cent. • gilt bronze with polychromy • 42.5 × 27 × 19 cm

First known previous owner: Max August Scipio von Brandt, imperial envoy in Beijing • Sold in 1883 to the Königliches Museum für Völkerkunde, Berlin (today: Staatliche Museen zu Berlin, Ethnologisches Museum, inv. no. I D 5752) • The object originates from a region that was partly under the influence of colonial powers from 1842 onwards. The possibility of unlawful acquisition cannot, therefore, be ruled out if it was put on the market after 1842.

The three-faced, eight-armed ***USHNISHAVIJAYA*** is the embodiment of an important Buddhist mantra that was believed to bring a prolongation of life and rebirth in Buddha Amitabha's 'Western Pure Land'.[8] Such protective mantras consist of sacred syllables that encapsulate the essence of Buddhist teaching. The bronze also holds relics – presumably sacred texts, medicinal herbs, votive tablets and the remains of a deceased teacher – that were deposited inside it in a special consecration ceremony. Only the ritual enhancement of these offerings gives it the power of benediction.[9] Except for the vase filled with the nectar of immortality and the double Vajra held to the breast, the figure has lost all its original attributes |see below|, the whereabouts of which are unknown. |BB|

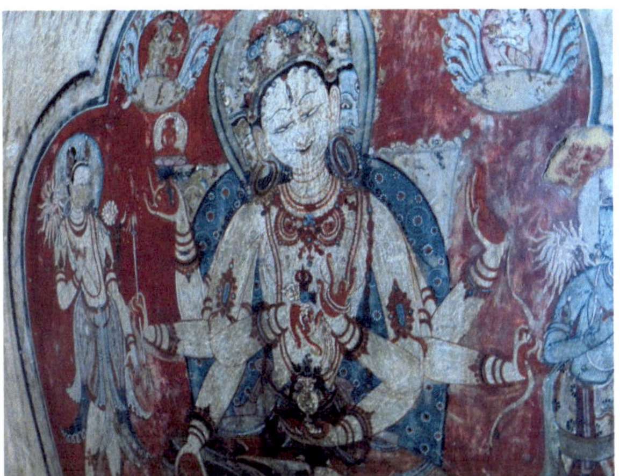

Ushnishavijaya with attributes. Detail of the painting on the stupa in the Luri Gompa in Mustang, Nepal, late 13th century, photograph from 2012

RELIQUARY FIGURE BWITI

Kota and Kélé region (Gabon or Republic of Congo) • 19th cent. • wood, copper, wire • 53 × 20 × 10.5 cm

Authors, users, custodians before European appropriation not documented • Oskar Lenz, from 1874–1877 geologist for the Afrikanische Gesellschaft Berlin on the River Ogowe (Gabon) • Assigned in 1877 to the Königliches Museum für Völkerkunde, Berlin (today: Staatliche Museen zu Berlin, Ethnologisches Museum, inv. no. III C 1088) • No evidence of unjust acquisition is known of at this time.

Preserving the remains of high-ranking ancestors served the Kota and Kélé as a means of communicating with the deceased and so strengthened the bonds connecting the living and the dead. This wooden corpus wound round with copper wire is a fragment of an ancestral altar. It shows a heavily stylised face that stands out clearly on account of its distinctive eyes and nose and would have been instantly recognizable to the initiated.[10] The lozenge-shaped appendage underneath the head would have been half-hidden in a reliquary filled with human remains and offerings, which would have been kept with others like it |see below|. European collectors often left such receptacles behind, despite their cultural value. The imported copper, which is also evidence of trade, transforms the reliquary figure into a symbol of wealth and power. |TS|

Illustration by Edouard Riou after a drawing by Jacques de Brazza. First published in 1887 as 'Voyages dans l'Ouest Africain' in the periodical *Le tour du monde: Nouveau journal des voyages*, edited by Pierre Savorgnan de Brazza and Edouard Charton. De Brazza made drawings to record what he saw of Africa in the course of his scientific expeditions. Through these drawings, the 'knowledge' of foreign customs and cultures that they supposedly conveyed could be published in magazines and so disseminated all over Europe.

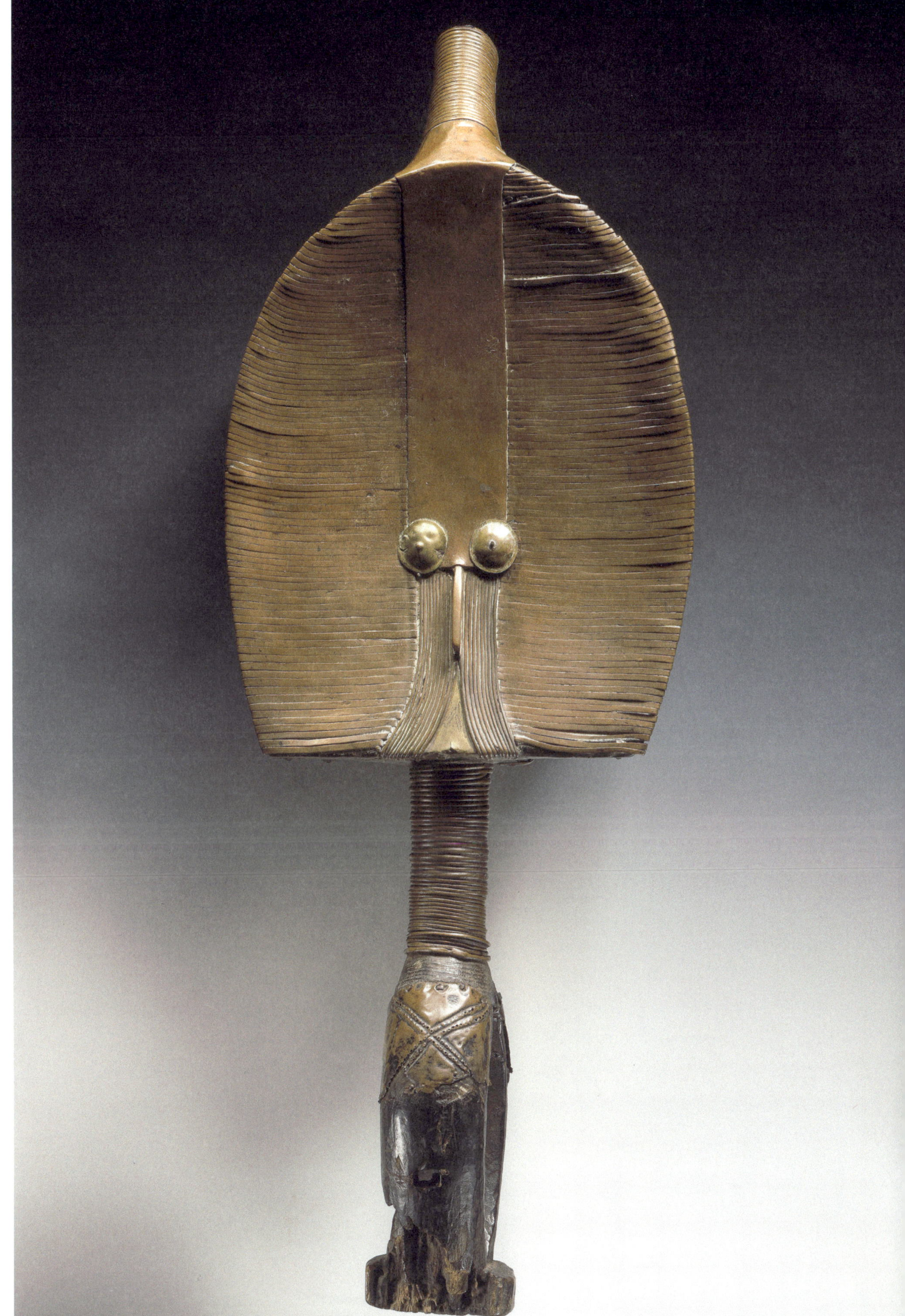

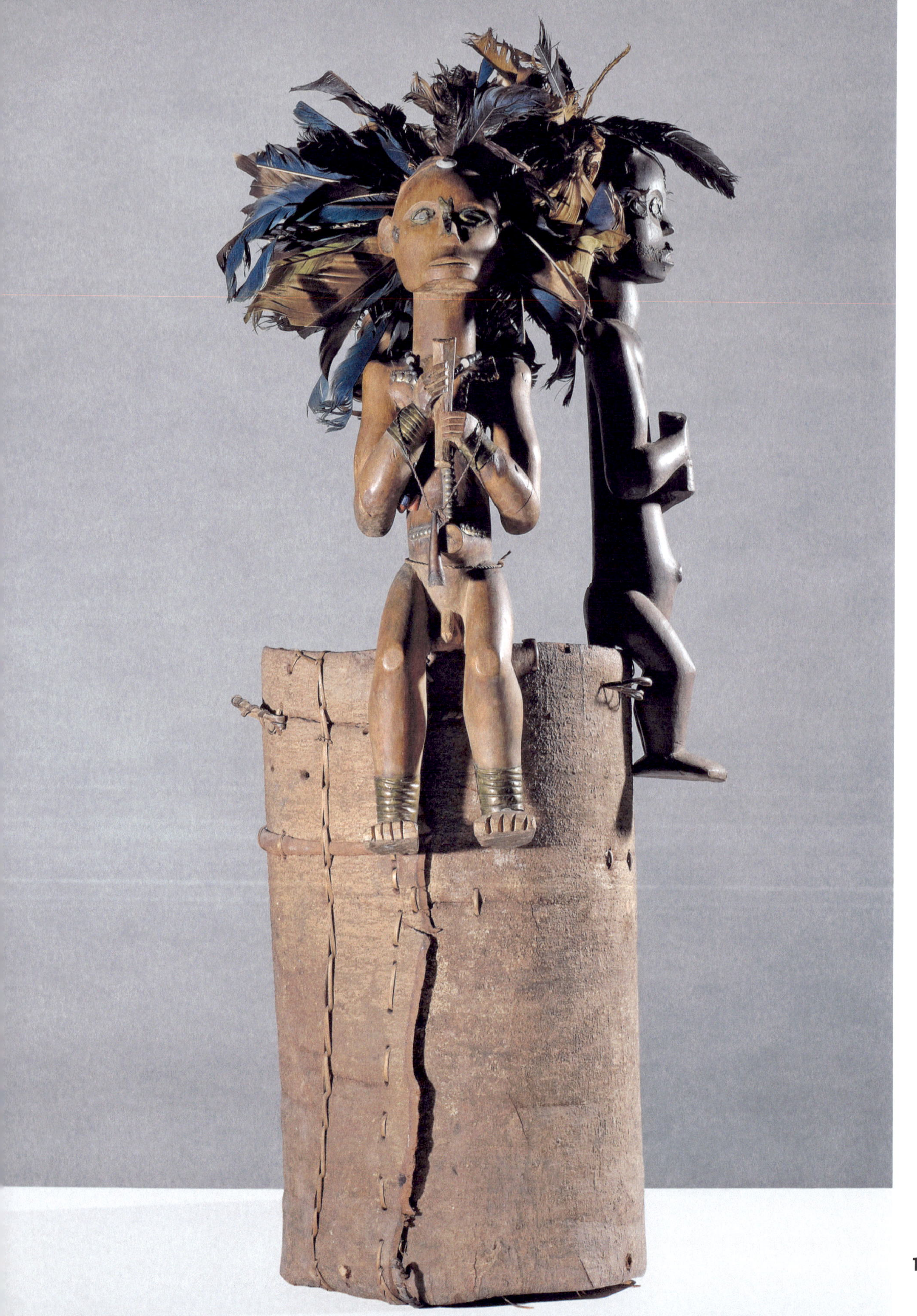

BYERI WITH RELIQUARY

Authors not documented •
Fang-Ngumba Region
(Cameroon) • 19th cent. •
wood, assorted feathers,
iron brass, glass, tree bark •
receptacle: 55 × 32 × 32 cm,
male figure: 59 × 51 × 16 cm
(without feathers), female
figure: 58 × 15 × 12 cm (without feathers)

Users, custodians before
European appropriation not
documented • Georg Zenker,
botanist, director of the
Jaunde station (Cameroon)
for the German Foreign
Office until 1895 • Sold in
1897 to the Königliches
Museum für Völkerkunde,
Berlin (today: Staatliche
Museen zu Berlin, Ethnologisches Museum, inv. no. III
C 6689 a–c) • The object
originates from a region
that at the time of its appropriation was under colonial
rule. We regard colonial-
ism as a context of systemic
injustice. Thus even gifts
and documented purchases
cannot invariably be re-
garded as having been lawfully acquired.

For the Fang-Ngumba in Cameroon, ancestors who had acquired high status on account of their exceptional skills, coura-
geous deeds or numerous progeny were deemed especially
helpful. To keep the connection to them alive, their skulls were
preserved in receptacles made of tree bark and worshipped.
The pair of figures on top of this receptacle guarded the human
remains inside it and warded off anyone who posed a threat.[11]
The pair's very striking appearance |see below| is a demonstra-
tion of the ancestor's power and would have kept women and
children, who were prohibited by social norms from coming too
close, at a distance. The reliquary ensemble marked a sacred
place.[12] |TS|

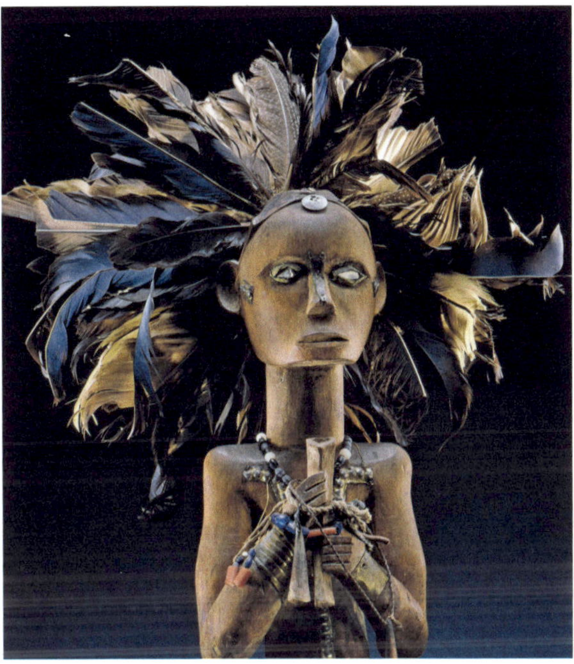

This photograph
shows details
of a *byeri*, magni-
ficently adorned
with real feathers,
brass appliqués
on the eyes and
breast, clasped
wrists and neck-
laces made of
coloured glass
beads

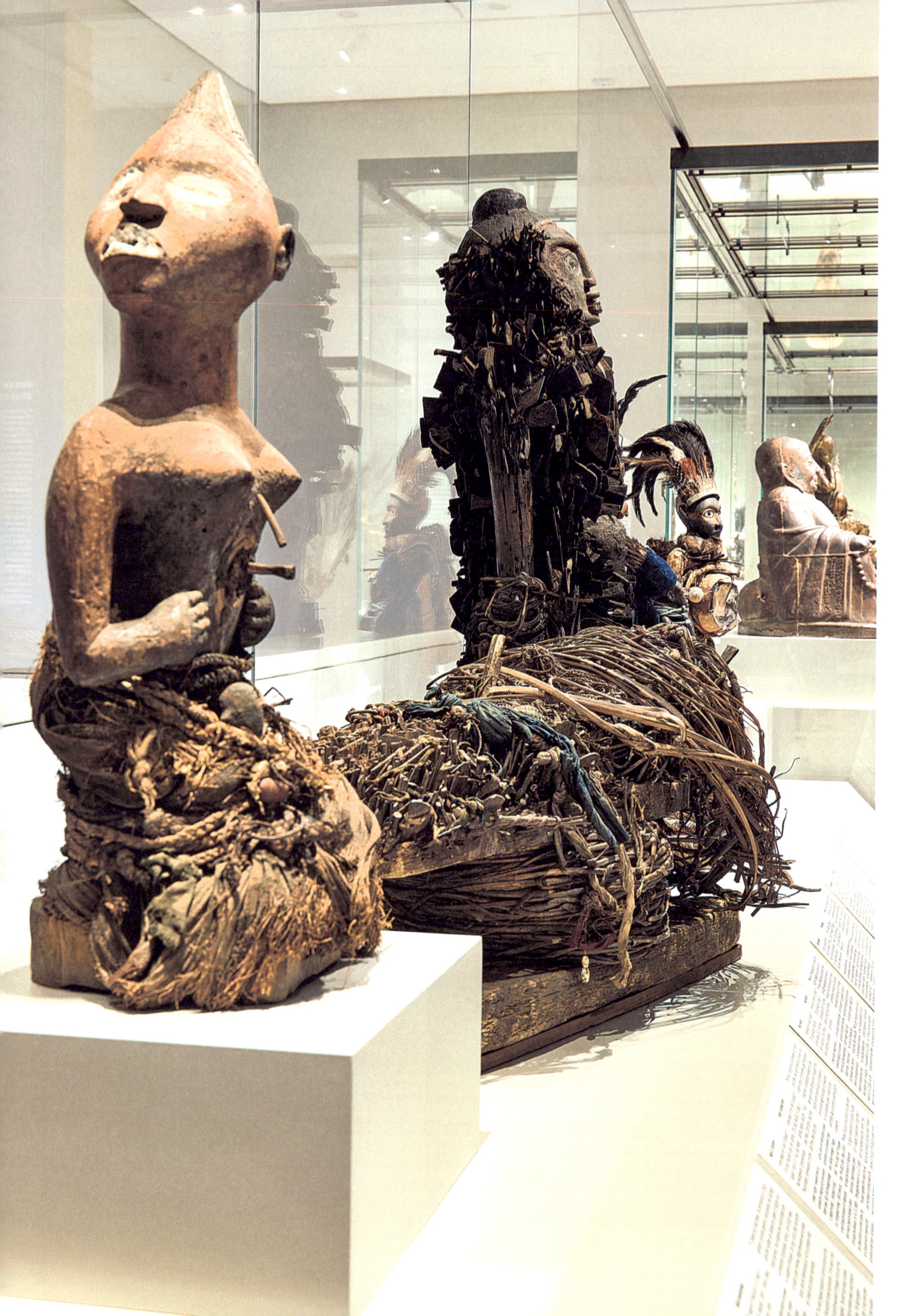

CHAPTER 4

CAN WORDS DESCRIBE THINGS?

The European museums that arose in the nineteenth century drew heavily on the taxonomic systems of the natural sciences. Objects were collected, evaluated and on the basis of certain key characteristics assigned to a museum of art or the history of culture, ethnography or natural history. There they were grouped together under one of the categories provided by the museum's own system of classification. The exhibits shown here were assigned to the categories 'power figures',[1] 'Buddhist deities' and 'depictions of Christ'. The selection illustrates just how quickly the limitations of those categories became apparent to anyone wishing to do justice to the complex and wide-ranging religious and cultural practices behind each object. The in-depth study of those same practices at the same time reveals how works belonging to the same object group can vary greatly in both design and use, as well as in the complexity of the concepts and worldviews associated with them. ———————

Museums are not neutral repositories. With their classifications and attributions, they have the power of definition and can construct images of cultures and religions that in many cases simply reinforce the Eurocentric worldview. These days we consider it important to present a less blinkered view. One way of doing that is to show the variety that exists within a given object group, or to transcend the pigeonholing effect of separate museum collections by rendering visible the many ways in which societies were and still are intertwined. |TS, BB| ———————

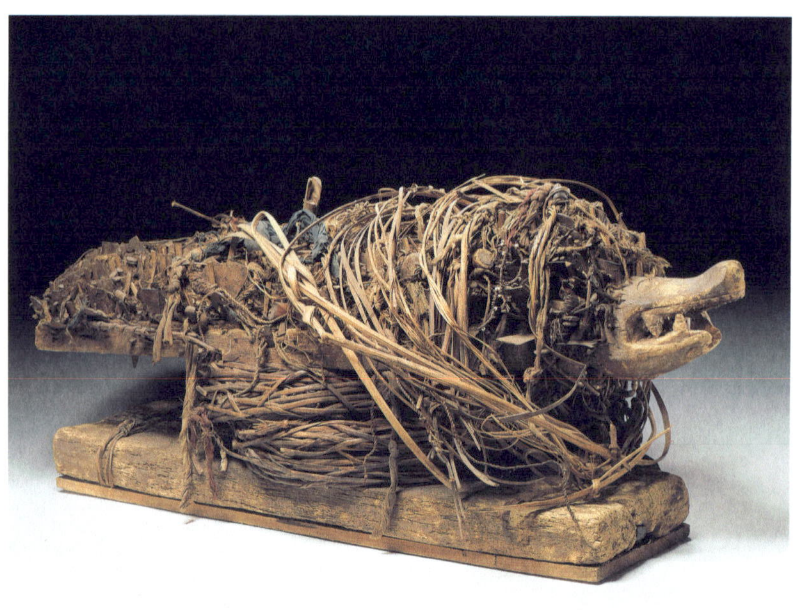

NKISI IN ANIMAL FORM

Authors not documented • Yombe region on the river Chiloango(?) (DR Congo, Republic of Congo or Cabinda, Angola) • End of 19th cent. • wood, glass, metal, cotton fabric, snail shells, plant fibres, seed pods, bone • 80 × 44 × 36 cm

Users, custodians before European appropriation not documented • Robert Visser, from 1882–1904 plantation manager in "Congo Free State", "French Congo" and "Portuguese Congo" • Gifted in 1904 to the Königliches Museum für Völkerkunde, Berlin (today: Staatliche Museen zu Berlin, Ethnologisches Museum, inv. no. III C 18905) • The object originates from a region that was under colonial rule at the time of its appropriation. We regard colonialism as a context of systemic Thus even gifts and documented purchases cannot invariably be regarded as having been lawfully acquired.

MINKISI (sing. *NKISI*) are vessels for non-human powers. This particular creation is reminiscent of a crocodile with frighteningly sharp teeth. Its wooden body is wrapped in several layers of plant fibres with dozens of metal parts tucked into them. Materials both natural and artificial had the capacity to turn the figure into a feared hunter capable of tracking down and repelling hostile forces.[2] It was these *BILONGO,* or empowering substances invested in the figure by expert ritualists,[3] that transformed *MINKISI* (sing. *NKISI*) into active players, while at the same time defining their outward appearance. |TS|

NKISI BANSIMBA

Authors not documented • Vili region(?) (DR Congo, Republic of Congo or Cabinda, Angola) 19th cent. • wood, glass, fabric, pigment, raffia • 58 × 33 × 24 cm

Users, custodians prior to European appropriation not documented • Robert Visser, from 1882–1904 plantation manager in "Congo Free State", "French Congo" and "Portuguese Congo" • Gifted in 1904 to the Königliches Museum für Völkerkunde, Berlin (today: Staatliche Museen zu Berlin, Ethnologisches Museum, inv. no. III C 18909) • The object originates from a region that was under colonial rule at the time of its appropriation. We regard colonialism as a context of systemic injustice. Thus even gifts and documented purchases cannot invariably be regarded as having been lawfully acquired.

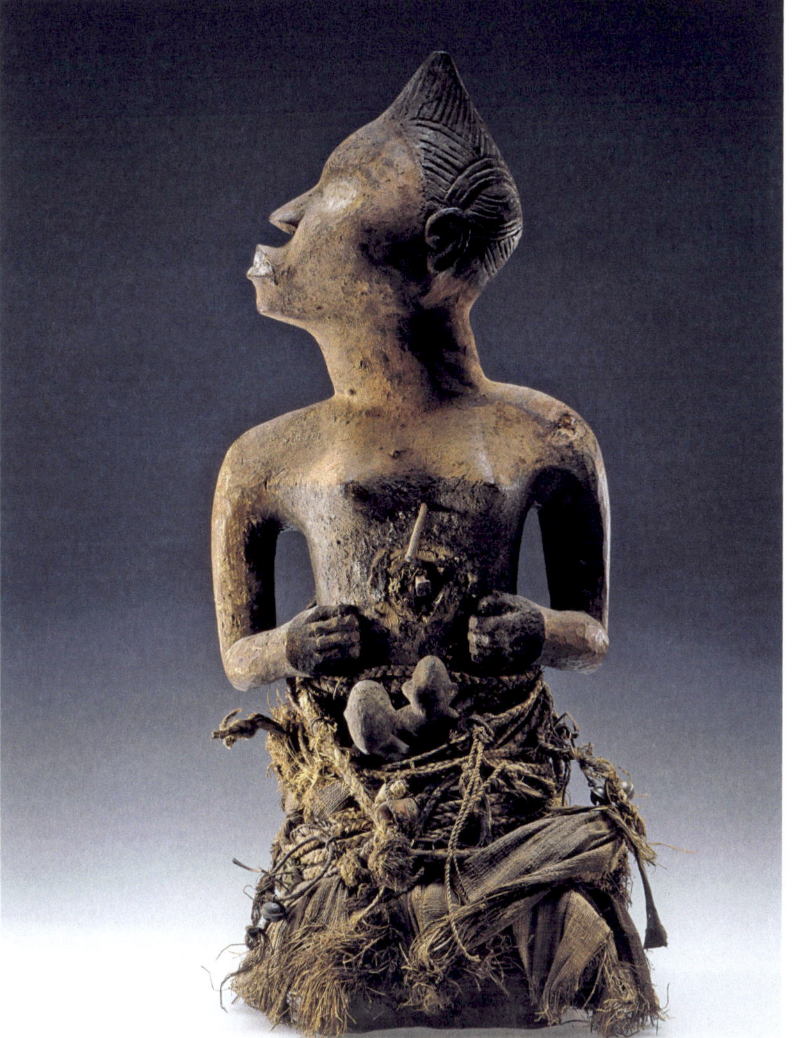

This **NKISI** forged a link to the tutelary spirits called **BANSIMBI**.[4] It was deployed at deliveries of twins to ward off the dangers for both mother and babies.[5] The lower half of the figure is wrapped in woven fabric, string, and raffia and has two doll-like figures popping out of its stomach. The skirt-like wrapping shields the empowering substances contained within it against external influences. The figure gazes heavenwards over her right shoulder, preventing direct eye contact. Perhaps this gesture connected the user to the invisible world of ancestors and spirits. |TS|

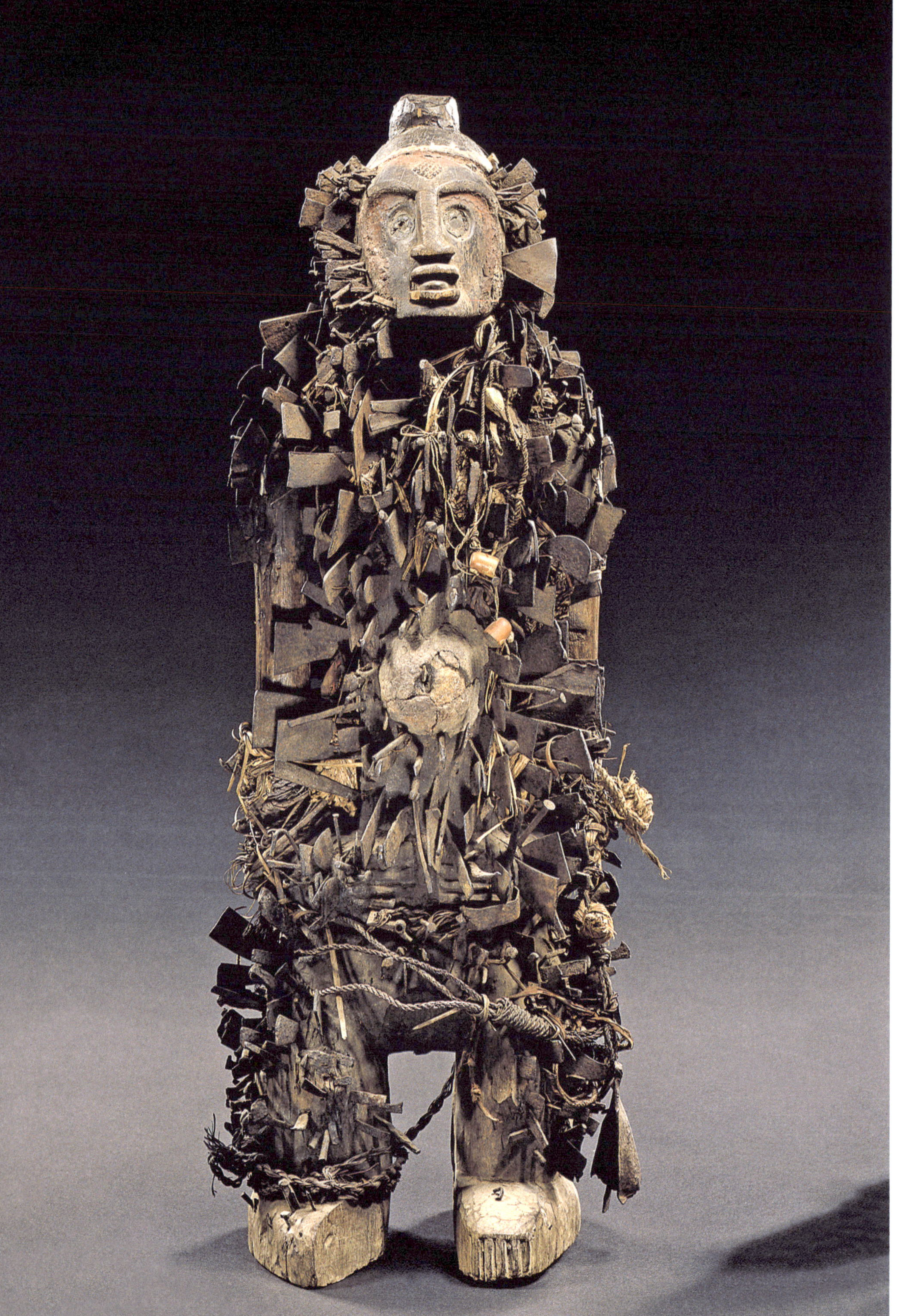

NKISI NKONDI

Authors not documented Yombe region on the river Chiloango(?) (DR Congo, Republic of Congo or Cabinda, Angola) • 19th cent. • wood, glass, feathers, nutshells, string, plant fibres, pigments, woven textiles • 87 × 36 × 29 cm

Authors, users, custodians before European appropriation undocumented • Robert Visser from 1882–1904 plantation manager in "Congo Free State", "French Congo" and "Portuguese Congo" • Gifted in 1904 to the Königliches Museum für Völkerkunde, Berlin (today: Staatliche Museen zu Berlin, Ethnologisches Museum, inv. no. III C 18914) • The object originates from a region that at the time of its appropriation was under colonial rule. We regard colonialism as a context of systemic injustice. Thus even gifts and documented purchases cannot invariably be regarded as having been lawfully acquired.

Among the Yombe, *ZINKONDI* (sing. *NKONDI*) witnessed agreements and administered justice. Contracts were rendered binding by driving nails and pieces of metal into the figure,[6] which is why this one is bristling with iron blades and nails. Interspersed among them are little medicine bags containing potent plant and animal substances. These were used by an expert ritualist called *NGANGA* to unleash powerful forces. The incredible potency of this *NKONDI,* as demonstrated by the large number of materials attached, could be directed against evildoers and anyone in breach of contract. |TS|

TSCHAMO SAME

Authors not documented • Vili and Yombe region, Brazzaville (Republic of Congo) • 19th cent. • dried gourd shell, dried fruit fibres, resin, cloth • 6.5 × 37 × 43 cm

Users, custodians before European appropriation not documented • Robert Visser, from 1882–1904 plantation manager in "Congo Free State", "French Congo" and "Portuguese Congo" • Gifted in 1898 to the Königliches Museum für Völkerkunde, Berlin (today: Staatliche Museen zu Berlin, Ethnologisches Museum, inv. no. III C 8104 b) • The object comes from a region that at the time of its appropriation was under colonial rule. We regard colonialism as a context of systemic injustice. Thus even gifts and documented purchases cannot invariably be regarded as having been lawfully acquired.

Out of respect for the sensitive character and function of these objects, we have chosen not to illustrate them here.

These two objects are shown here as examples of non-representational, 'aniconic' *MINKISI*. They owe their efficacy to the belief that they could invoke or ward off evil forces. In a brief note on their use, plantation manager Robert Visser described them as very old and greatly feared[7] |p. 51|. The extent to which he himself believed in their potency or saw them as objects of 'superstition' is not recorded.

Hidden inside the *TSCHAMO SAME* are vegetable and artificial substances with the aid of which a *NGANGA*, according to some stories, could invoke or avert death.[8] No detailed descriptions of these practices have been handed down to us. |TS|

The register of accessions to the Königliches Museum für Völkerkunde records only the most cursory information about the objects entering the museum.

19

TSCHAMO SAME

Authors not documented • Vili and Yombe region, Brazzaville (Republic of Congo) • 19th cent. • calabash, cloth, metal • 23 × 16 × 16 cm

Users, custodians before European appropriation not documented • Robert Visser, from 1882–1904 plantation manager in "Congo Free State", "French Congo" and "Portuguese Congo" • Gifted in 1898 to the Königliches Museum für Völkerkunde, Berlin (today: Staatliche Museen zu Berlin, Ethnologisches Museum, inv. no. III C 8104 c) • The object comes from a region that at the time of its appropriation was under colonial rule. We regard colonialism as a context of systemic injustice. Thus even gifts and documented purchases cannot invariably be regarded as having been lawfully acquired.

NKISI LUMWENO

Authors not documented • Vili region, Kingdom of Loango, Loango coast (Republic of Congo) • 19th cent. • wood, glass, cotton fabric, velvet, feathers • 33 × 11 × 27 cm

Users, custodians before European appropriation not documented • Fritz Klingelhöfer(?), companion of Adolf Bastians (first director of the Königliches Museum für Völkerkunde, Berlin) on the German expedition to the Loango coast (1873–74), financed by the Afrikanische Gesellschaft Berlin • In 1875, taken into the Königliches Museum für Völkerkunde, Berlin (today: Staatliche Museen zu Berlin, Ethnologiisches Museum, inv. no. III C 531) •

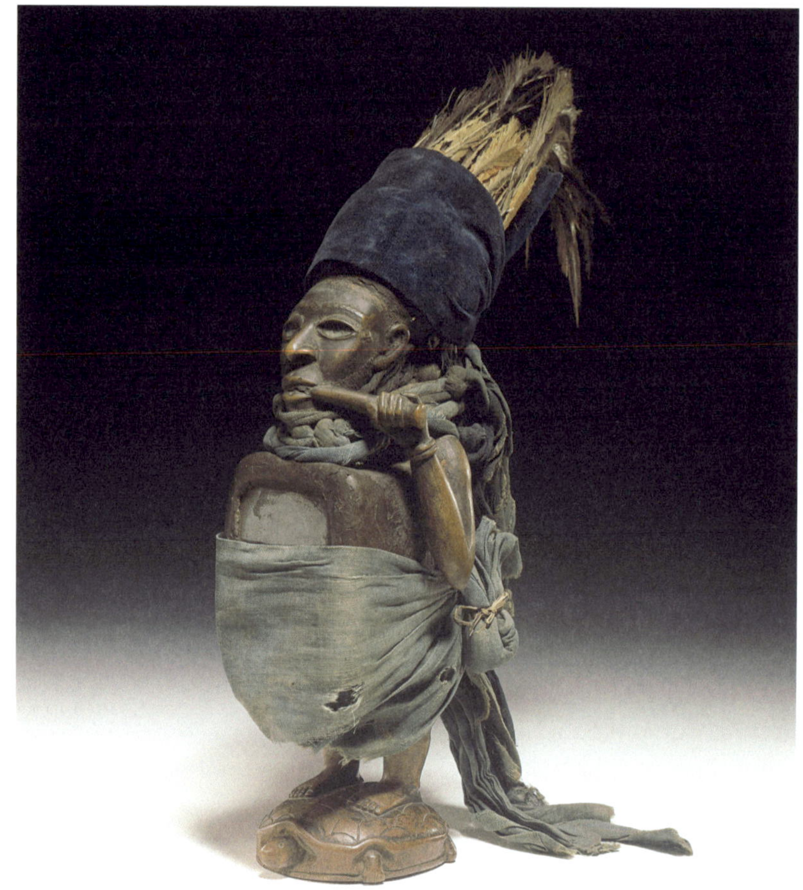

The figure standing on a tortoise wears a feather headdress with a strip of velvet tied around it. The centrepiece of the object is the mirror half hidden behind a cloth sheath that would have served the **NGANGA** as a bridge to the world of ancestors and spirits. The tortoise, as a creature regarded by various communities all along the Loango coast as a wanderer between the worlds,[9] also forged such a link. The several layers of knotted textiles wrapped around the wooden corpus were added gradually and indicate that the figure was used actively in rituals over a long period. |TS|

NKISI LUMWENO

Authors not documented • Vili region, Loango coast(?) (Republic of Congo) • 19th cent. • wood, mirrored glass, cardboard, iron, metal bell, cloth, fur, feathers, plant fibres, resin • 53 × 19 × 27 cm

Users, custodians before European appropriation not documented • Robert Visser, from 1882–1904 plantation manager in "Congo Free State", "French Congo" and "Portuguese Congo" • Gifted in 1898 to the Königliches Museum für Völkerkunde, Berlin (today: Staatliche Museen zu Berlin, Ethnologisches Museum, inv. no. III C 8105) • The object comes from a region that at the time of its appropriation was under colonial rule. We regard colonialism as a context of systemic injustice. Thus even gifts and documented purchases cannot invariably be regarded as having been lawfully acquired.

21

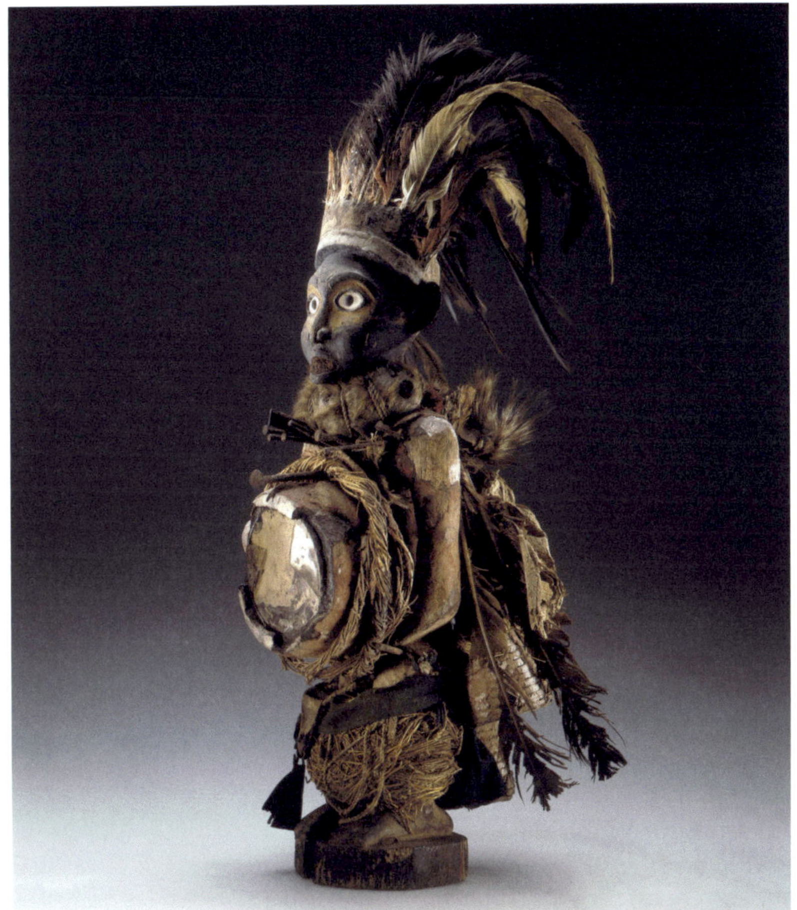

The figure created to protect against malevolent forces stares back at us with wide-open eyes. The red-rimmed eyes, feather headdress and fur-trimmed cape identify it as a hunter who could track down and ward off threats.[10] Projecting from its stomach is the *LUMWENO*, a mirror which by virtue of its capacity for reflection spots dangerous forces and at the same time affords the expert ritualist a glimpse of the 'other' world.[11] The striking rendition of the eyes is an allusion to the figure's powers of prophecy. By attaching powerful medicine bags (*BILONGO*) to the figure, the *NGANGA* could endow it with healing powers too |see below|. |TS|

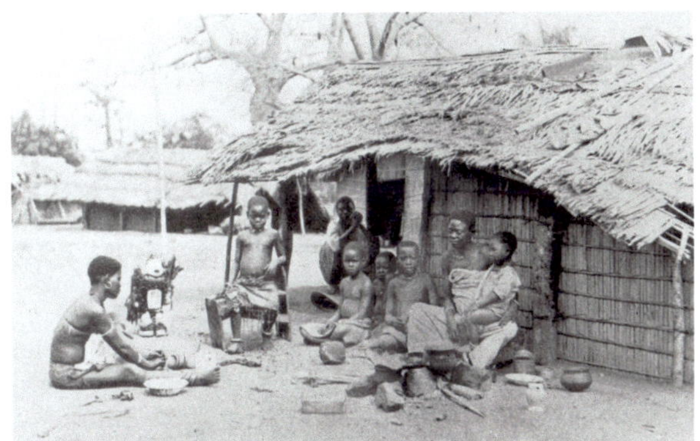

This photograph by Da Cunha Moraes shows a female nganga – perhaps preparing the powerful medicine called bilongo. First published in *Africa Occidental: Album photographico e descriptivo*, 1885

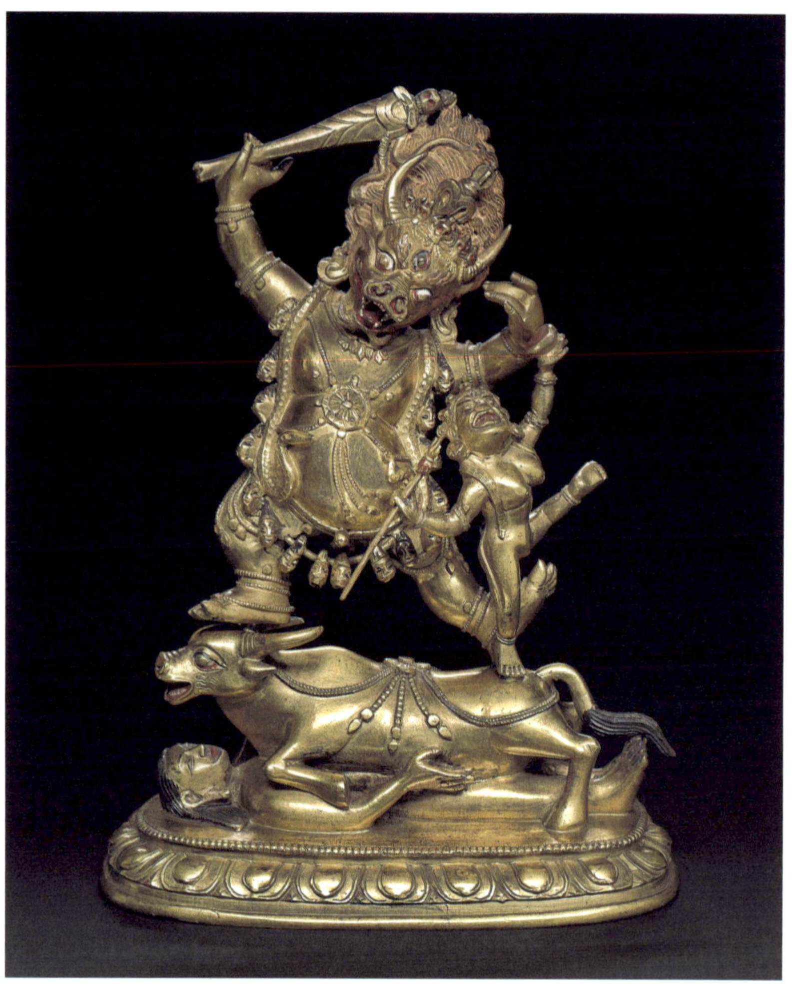

Author not documented •
(Mongolia) • 18th cent. • gilt
bronze, tripartite, pigments •
18 × 13.6 × 6.6 cm

First known previous owner:
Paul Dahms • Purchased
in 1964 by Ludolf Lülfing on
behalf of the Museum für
Völkerkunde, Berlin (today:
Staatliche Museen zu Berlin,
Ethnologisches Museum,
inv. no. I D 37617 a) • No evidence of unjust acquisition
is known of at this time.

Enlightened beings (Bodhisattva) can take on terrifying forms.
The buffalo-headed ***YAMA DHARMARAJA*** is a wrathful embodiment of the Bodhisattva Manjushri. He is the conqueror of
death, who in India and elsewhere is imagined as a buffalo.[12]
Here, Yama Dharmaraja is shown in mid-stride with his wisdom partner Chamundi, standing on a bellowing buffalo and
swinging his club. In his ignorance, the dying man beneath
him is overwhelmed by death, and consequently reborn. The
radical symbolism of the figure visualises the striving for en-
lightenment that will put an end to the cycle of rebirth. |BB|

DAMASK CLOAK OF YAMA DHARMARAJA

Authors not documented • (Mongolia) • Probably 19th cent. • 25 × 24 × 0.2 cm

Possible previous owners unknown • In 1964, purchased by Ludolf Lülfing on behalf of the Museum für Völkerkunde, Berlin (today: Staatliche Museen zu Berlin, Ethnologisches Museum, inv. no. I D 37617 b) • No evidence of unjust acquisition is known of at this time.

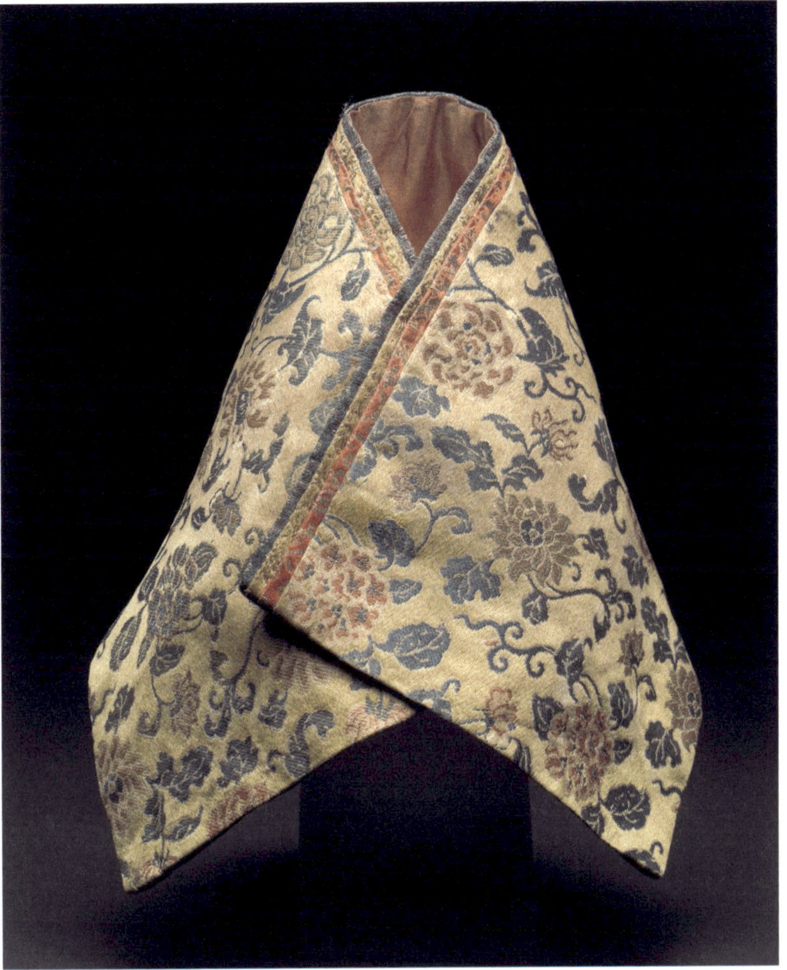

Buddhist deities, whose complex or terrifying iconography was intelligible only to initiated monks, were usually kept in sealed rooms inside a temple and swathed in cloaks |see below| to conceal their attributes from the public.[13] |BB|

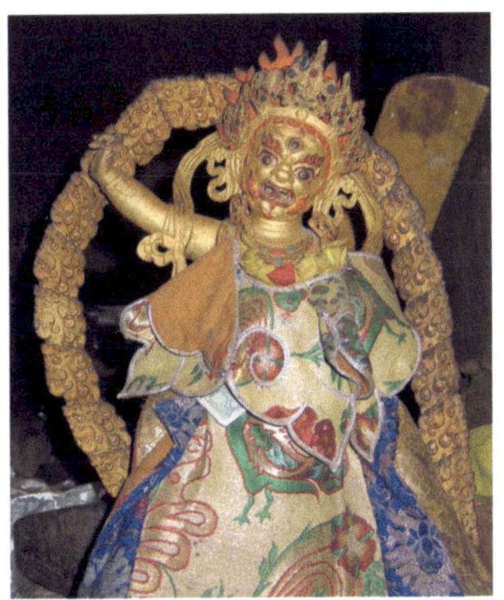

Clothed wrathful deity in the Nyethang Temple, Tibet

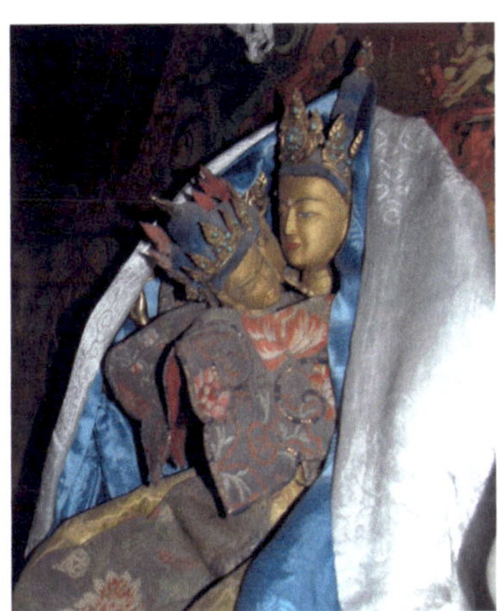

Clothed Buddhist initiation deity united with her partner wisdom, Norbulingka Palace, Lhasa, Tibet

BODHISATTVA MAHASTHAMAPRAPTA

Author not documented •
Dolonor, Inner Mongolia
(China) • 19th cent. •
gilt bronze with pigments,
malachite, solid cast •
29.5 × 11 × 11.2 cm

First known previous owner:
Heinrich Peters • Sold in
1959 to the Museum für Völkerkunde, Berlin (today:
Staatliche Museen zu Berlin,
Ethnologisches Museum,
inv. no. I D 36823) • No
evidence of unjust acquisition is known of at this time.

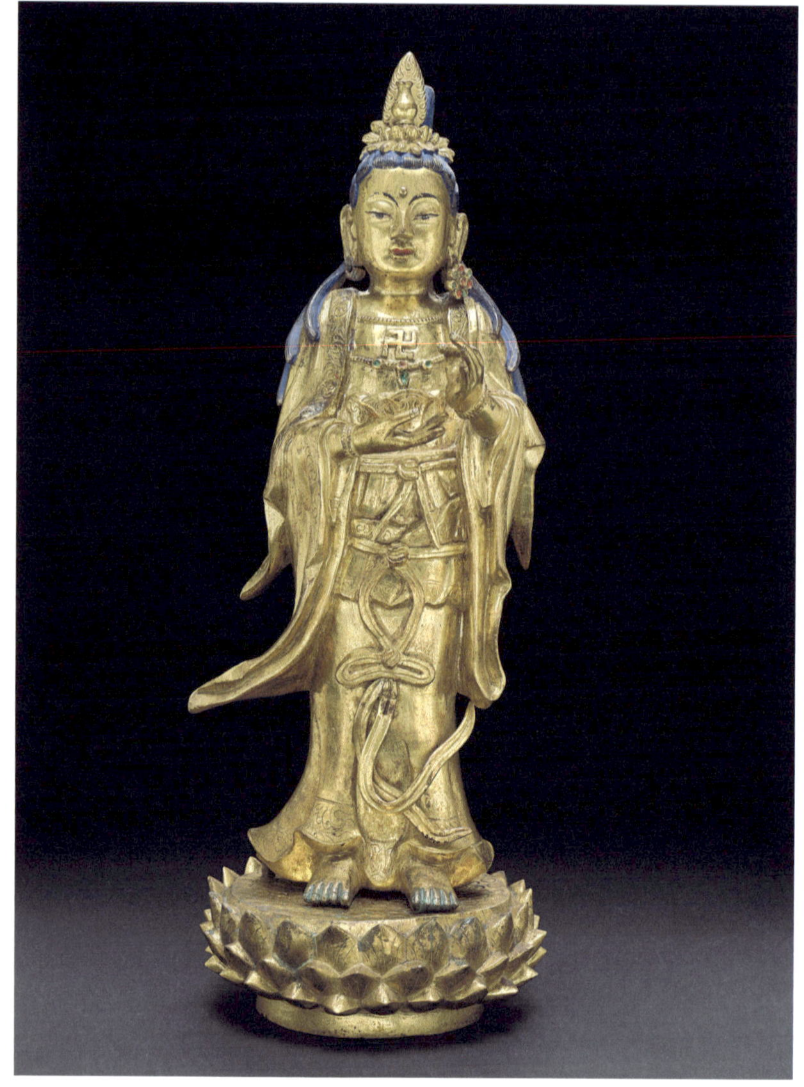

24

The ***BODHISATTVA MAHASTHAMAPRAPTA*** is one of two figures accompanying the cosmic Buddha Amitabha and represents the Buddha's strength and wisdom.[14] Decked out like
a prince, he stands on a lotus. His attribute is the vase on his
headdress, while blazoned on his chest is an auspicious swas-
tika emblem. The lotus flower that he originally held by the
stem in both hands is missing, its whereabouts unknown.
Together with ***BODHISATTVA AVALOKITESHVARA*** |see p. 83|
Bodhisattva Mahasthamaprapta guides the dead to Buddha
Amitabha's 'Western Pure Land', a spiritual place of refuge that
ends the sorrowful cycle of rebirth. |BB|

MANI STONE

Author not documented • Tibet (China) or Sikkim (India) • 19th cent. • stone with finely engraved Tibetan protective mantra • 27 × 18 cm

First known previous owner: Hermann von Schlagintweit, explorer of the Himalayas and geologist • Sold in 1882 to the Museum für Völkerkunde, Berlin (today: Staatliche Museen zu Berlin, Ethnologisches Museum, inv. no. I D 4865) • No evidence of unjust acquisition is known of at this time.

25

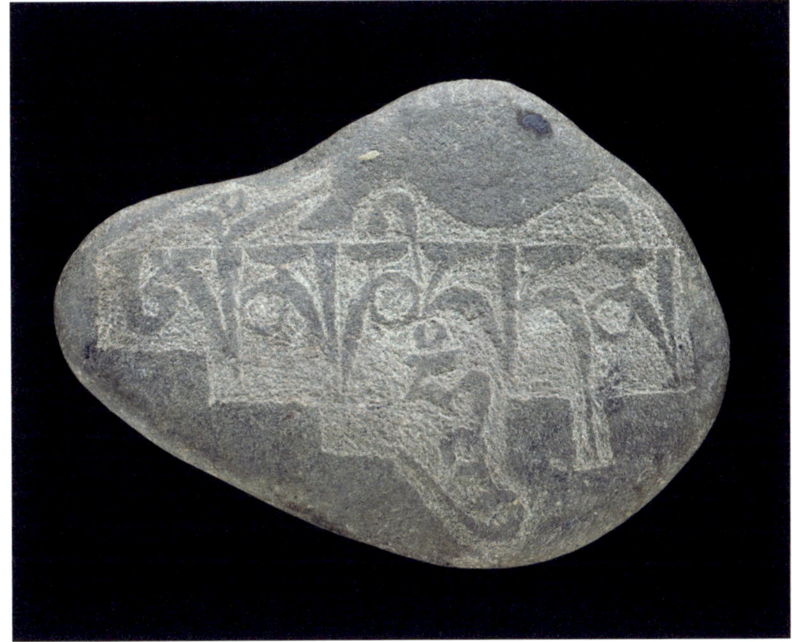

The stone bears a Tibetan engraving of the six-syllable Buddhist mantra 'Om mani padme hum', representing the essence of the ***BODHISATTVA AVALOKITESHVARA*** |see p. 83|. This inscription makes the stone a sacred jewel, or ***MANI***, attesting to the presence of the Bodhisattva Avalokiteshvara in the world.[15] ***MANI*** stones with engraved mantras are placed on the wayside as sacrificial offerings, but are also piled into cairns on mountain passes |see below| or used to build stone walls near monasteries. Their presence sanctifies the inhospitable environment of the Tibetan Plateau and bestows protection and blessings on those who travel there. |BB|

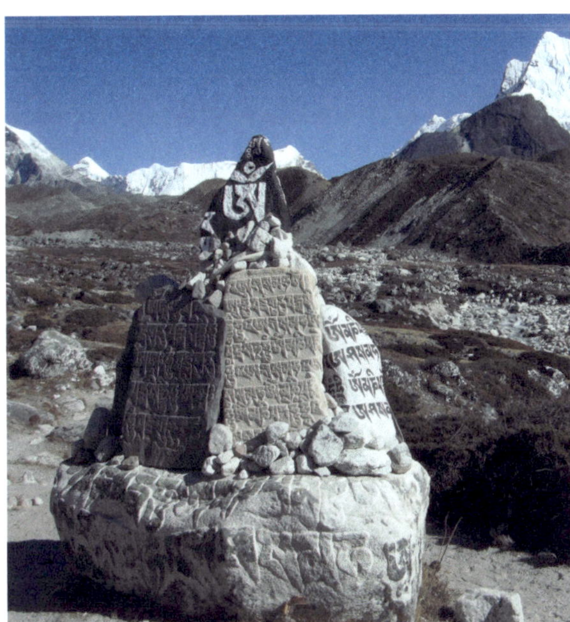

Cairn of mani stones, Khumbu Himal, Nepal, photograph of 2007

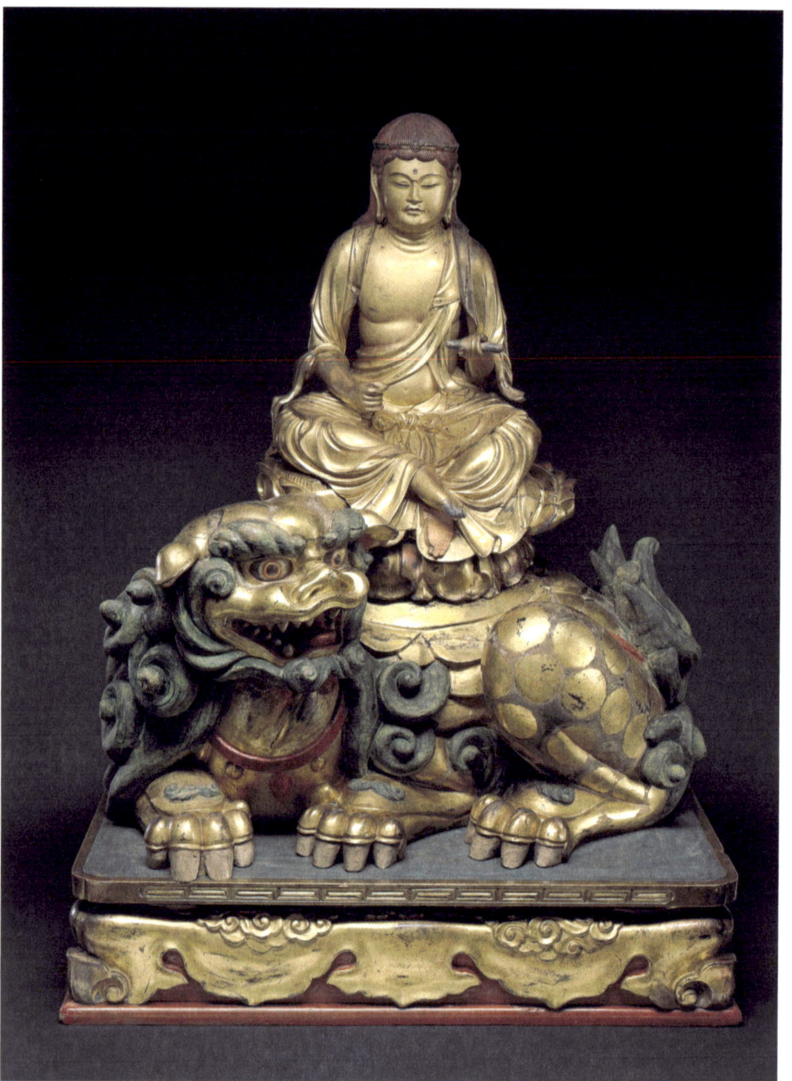

MANJUSHRI ON HIS LION

Author not documented •
(Japan) • c. 1800 • wood
with gilding, dry lacquer,
and polychromy, glass •
81 × 63 × 44 cm

Possible previous owners
unknown • Purchased
in 1907 by Adolf Fischer,
attaché and art expert
to the Imperial German
delegation in Beijing (China)
on behalf of the König-
liches Museum für Völker-
kunde Berlin (today: Staatliche Museen zu Berlin,
Ethnologisches Museum,
inv. no. I D 27245) • No
evidence of unjust acquisition is known of at this time.

BODHISATTVA MANJUSHRI is revered as a mentor and teacher who helps believers in their quest for knowledge. Unadorned
and with his long hair hanging loose, Manjushri – whose name
means 'graceful and venerable' – sits casually on his lion. As
an embodiment of the wisdom of the Buddha, he holds a scroll
in his left hand. The sword that he originally held in his right
hand for symbolically slashing through the fog of ignorance
preventing enlightenment has been lost. The aureole behind
his head and back is also missing. This form of representation
arose in Japan and is based on the *MANJUSHRI-PARINIR-
VANA-SUTRA*, according to which the Bodhisattva Manjushri
can also appear to the faithful as an orphaned child or beg-
gar.[16] The various parts of the ensemble were probably made
in different workshops. |BB|

BODHISATTVA KSHITIGARBHA

Author not documented •
(Japan) • c. 1850 • Wood
with gilding, dry lacquer,
and polychromy, metal •
65.5 × 38.5 × 34.5 cm

First known previous
owner: Mrs. Rummel • Sold
in 1916 to the Königliches
Museum für Völkerkunde,
Berlin (today: Staatliche
Museen zu Berlin, Ethnologisches Museum, inv. no.
I D 27750 a–c) • No evi-
dence of unjust acquisition
is known of at this time.

The ***BODHISATTVA KSHITIGARBHA*** is depicted as a monk
with shaven head. Supporting his head with his right hand, he
sits in a relaxed pose on a lotus throne in a rocky landscape.
His almost closed eyes indicate that he is deep in the medita-
tion by which he will liberate the dead from hell and lead them
to Buddha Amitabha's 'Western Pure Land'.[17] Three flaming
wish-fulfilling jewels adorn his nimbus. His other attributes,
specifically the wish-fulfilling jewel that he once held in his
left hand and his pilgrim's staff with rattle, are missing. Their
whereabouts are unknown. |BB|

27

BUDAI HESHANG

Author not documented •
Shanxi (China) • 17th cent. •
cast iron with traces of
gold paint and the donor's
engraved inscription •
61 × 59.5 × 62.5 cm

First known previous owner:
Paul Wegener, from 1906–
1948 actor for the stage and
screen in Berlin • In 1958,
gifted from Wegener's es-
tate to the Museum für
Völkerkunde, Berlin (today:
Staatliche Museen zu Berlin,
Ethnologisches Museum,
inv. no. I D 36843) • The object originates from a region
that was partly under the
influence of colonial powers
from 1842 onwards. The
possibility of unlawful acquisition cannot, therefore, be
ruled out if it was put on the
market after 1842.

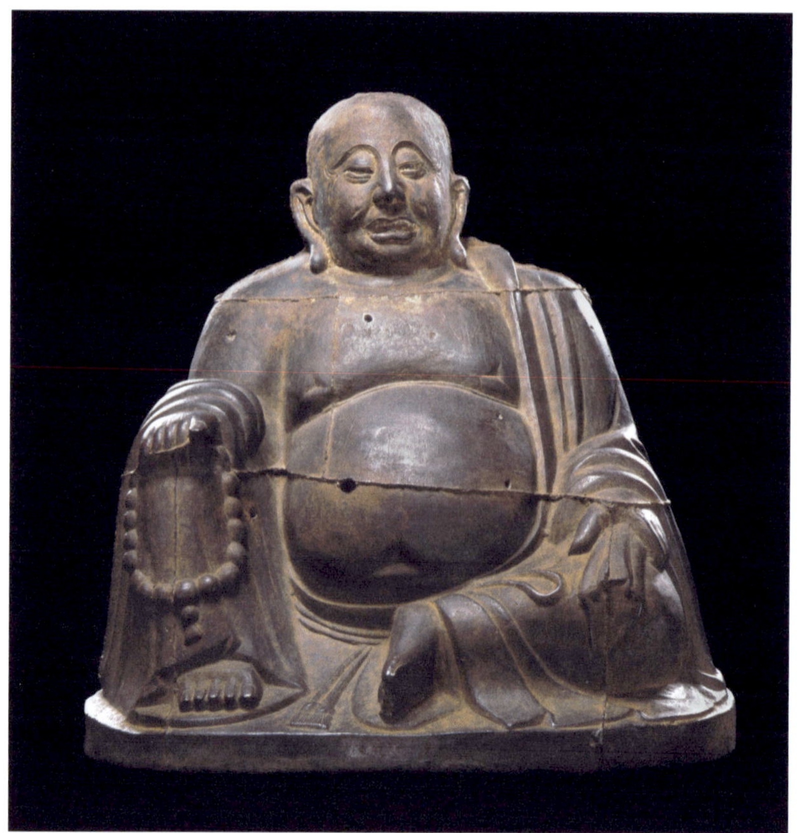

28

In *MAHAYANA* Buddhism, even historical individuals are regarded as reincarnations of an enlightened being or *BODHI-
SATTVA*.[18] *BUDAI HESHANG* (the monk with hempen bag,
ninth cent.) is regarded as the embodiment of the future Buddha Maitreya and has remained one of East Asia's most pop-
ular Buddhist saviour figures to this day |see below|. With his big
belly and tattered clothes, he is depicted as a laughing vaga-
bond who lives from day to day and has no interest in studying sacred texts. Thus, he challenges the ascetic ideal of the
studious monk and shows that enlightenment and liberation
from the cycle of rebirth are possible, even without adherence
to strict rules. |BB|

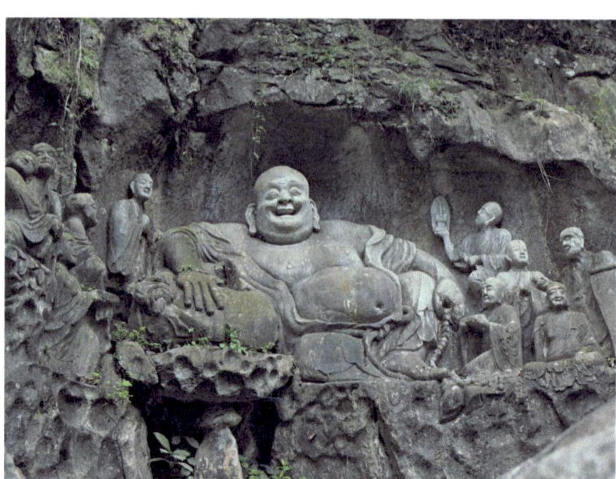

Monumental relief
sculpture of Bu-
dai Heshang with
18 Arhats, Feilai-
feng, Hangzhou,
China, 13th century,
photograph of
2012

CRUCIFIX

Authors not documented •
Kingdom of Kongo
(DR Congo and Angola) •
16th–18th cent. (?) • brass •
31.2 × 15.5 × 2.6 cm

Users, custodians before
European appropriation
not documented • Charles
Jacques Massar • Sold
in 1987 to the Staatliche
Museen zu Berlin, Museum
für Völkerkunde (today:
Staatliche Museen zu Berlin,
Ethnologisches Museum,
inv. no. III C 44815) •

This crucifix is a sign of the adoption of Christianity by the rulers of the Kingdom of Kongo following their first contact with the Portuguese in the late fifteenth century. The transcontinental alliance that arose was reinforced with artefacts commissioned by the Congolese elite.

The work exhibited here combines a European language of forms with a Central African worldview. While it draws on the iconographic conventions of Portuguese, Spanish and Italian crucifixes of this period, the symbolism presents a distinctly Congolese version of Christ's sacrifice,[19] as is borne out by the three praying figures surrounding Jesus. The lozenge-shaped indentations on the four termini of the cross probably point to its regional significance as a symbol of the cosmos. Starting in the eighteenth century, crucifixes – divorced from their Christian function – became important attributes of power in the Congolese context.[20] |TS|

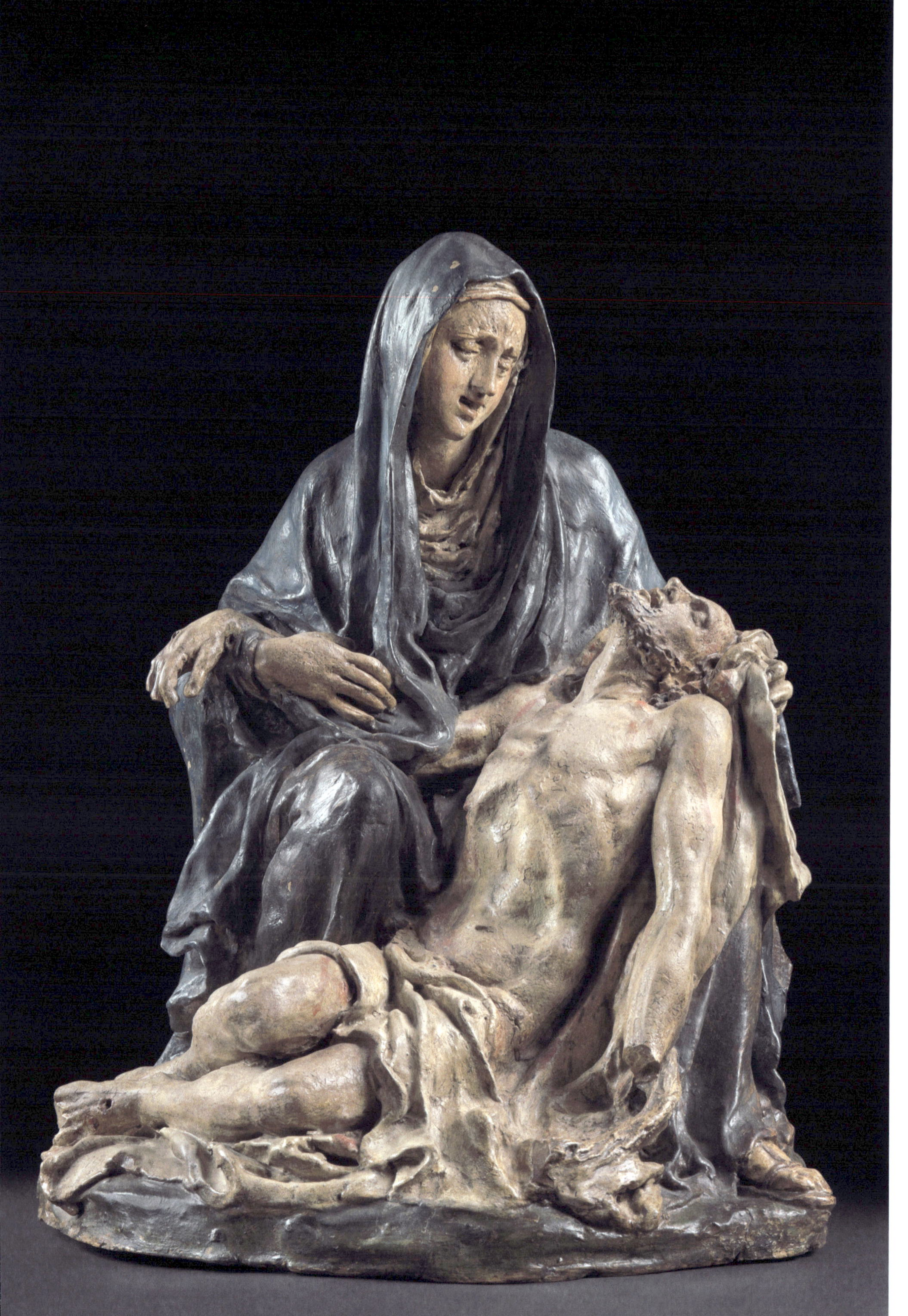

MARY WITH DEAD CHRIST (PIETÀ)

Author not documented •
(Spain) • 1680–1700 •
painted terracotta •
43 × 34 × 32 cm

First known previous owner:
Franz Rademacher, art
historian and director of the
Rheinisches Landesmuseum
Bonn, as a member of the
NSDAP from 1933–1945 com-
plicit in the Nazis' theft
of works of art from France,
Belgium and the Nether-
lands • Gifted in 1984 to the
Staatliche Museen zu
Berlin, Skulpturensammlung,
inv. no. 8/84 • The object
was quite possibly acquired
in a region that at the time
of its appropriation was
under Nazi rule. An unlawful
acquisition cannot, therefore, be ruled out.

There is no mention in the Gospels of Mary cradling the dead Christ in her lap after the deposition from the cross. The visu-alisations of this event referred to a Pietà (Italian for 'pity') or known by the German term *Vesperbild*, grew out of develop-ments in medieval piety. Their focus on the suffering figure of Christ and the anguish of his mother Mary were an emotive appeal to the faithful to empathise with these two key protag-onists of the Christian faith.[21]

The trend reached its apogee in the hyper-realistic, life-sized depictions of Mary and her son that emerged in seventeenth-century Spain and that even today are still carried out onto the streets as part of the Holy Week processions |see below|. With its haunting image of Christ's sufferings this smaller Pietà was probably created for private devotions. |JC|

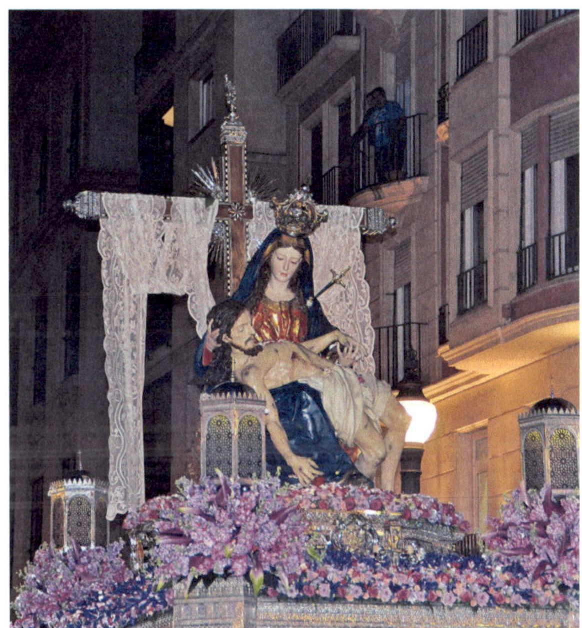

A Pietà held aloft during a Semana Santa (Holy Week) procession in Granada, Anda-lusia, Spain. Torcuato Ruiz del Peral, *Mother of Sorrows*, 1750, wood carving with polychromy, Iglesia de Santa María de la Encar-nación de la Al-hambra, Granada

THE BLESSING CHRIST CHILD

Monogrammed J. v. B. •
Southern Germany • 1567 •
Solnhofen limestone •
18 × 12.8 × 2.6 cm

First known previous owner:
Benoit Oppenheim, c. 1900
banker in Berlin • Sold in
1930 to the Kaiser Friedrich
Museumsverein (today:
Staatliche Museen zu Berlin,
Skulpturensammlung und
Museum für Byzantinische
Kunst, property of the Kaiser
Friedrich Museumsverein,
Berlin, inv. no. M 185) • No
evidence of unjust acquisi-
tion is known of at this time.

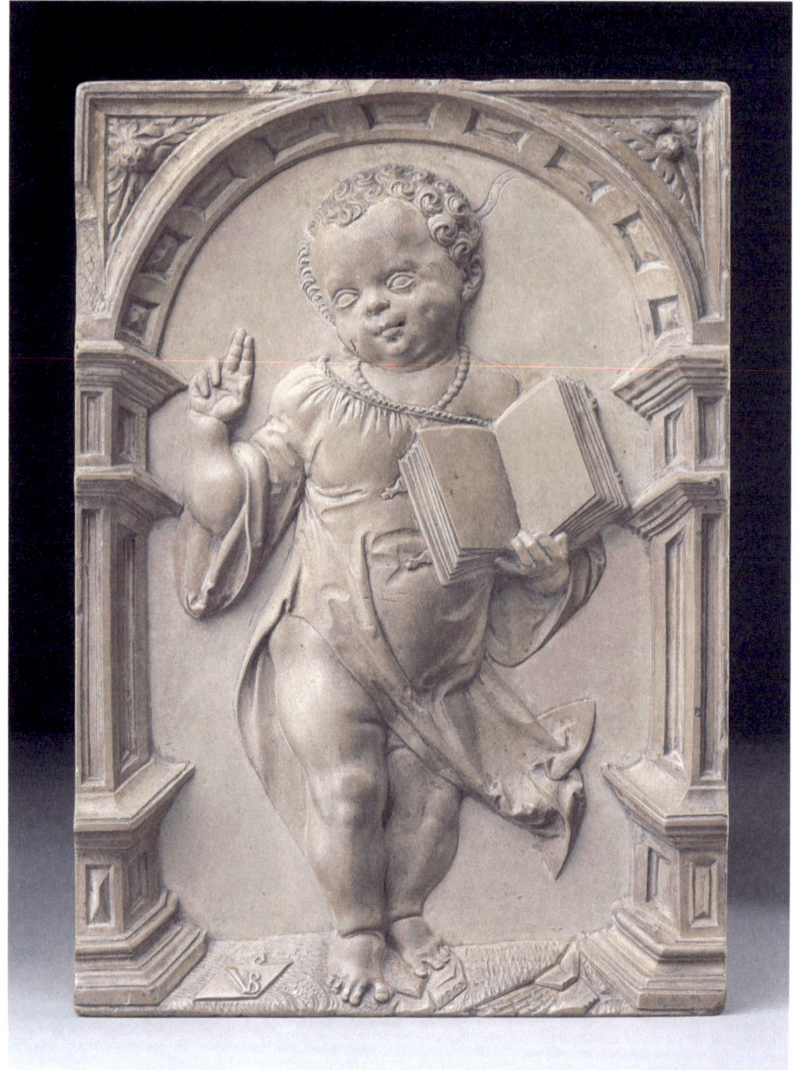

The architectural frame resembling a triumphal arch is almost completely filled by the figure of the Christ Child with his right hand raised in blessing. He wears a necklace and a loose-fitting tunic, billowing in the wind. The open book that he holds out towards the viewer identifies the infant Jesus as the *Logos*, that is, as the proclaimer of the Word of God.[22]

The material, Solnhofen limestone, lent itself to very detailed modelling and subsequent polishing. Especially ingenious is the impression created of a fully three-dimensional figure, despite the flatness of the relief. While the curls of hair on the front and top of the boy's head are modelled in the round, on the right-hand side they are incised into the background. The type of the chubby child, also known as a *Putto*, entered German iconography from Italy in the early sixteenth century. The gesture of blessing, the book and the tunic identify the figure as Jesus.[23] Without these attributes the little boy might be read as a secular or mythological motif. |JC|

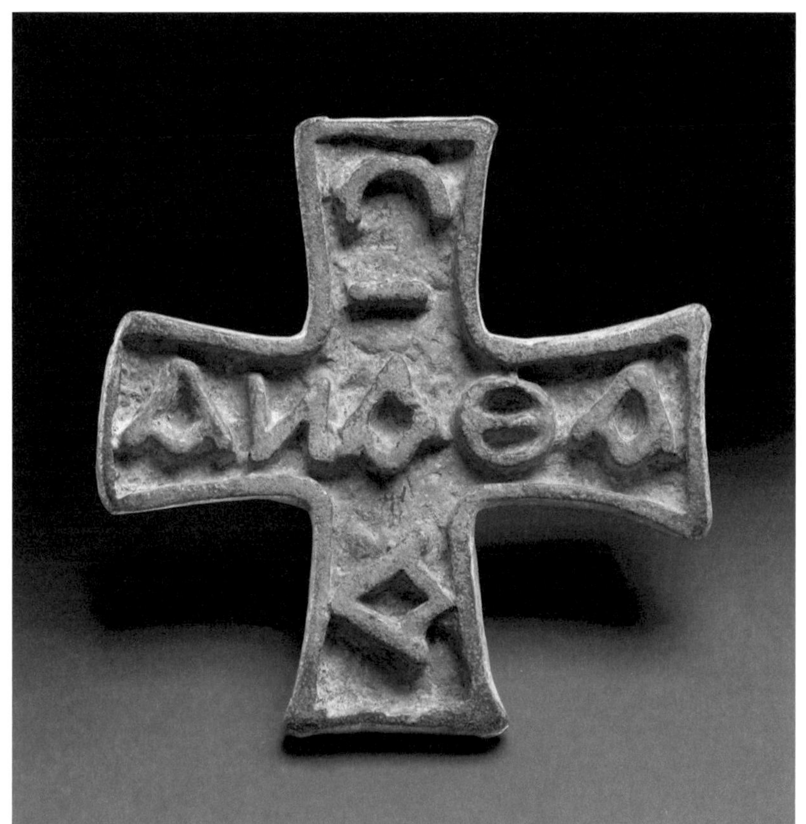

32

**STAMP WITH
GREEK INSCRIPTION**

Author not documented •
Eastern Mediterranean •
301–600 • Bronze •
3.9 × 8.5 × 8.6 cm

First known previous owner:
Saeed Motamed, in the
1960s–1990s art dealer in
Frankfurt am Main • Sold
in 1972 to the Frühchristlich-
Byzantinische Sammlung,
Berlin (today: Staatliche Museen zu Berlin, Skulpturensammlung und Museum für
Byzantinische Kunst, inv.
no. 8/72) • No evidence of
unjust acquisition is known
of at this time.

Stamps were used in many areas of daily life in Late Antiquity. The imprint of a stamp might identify the owner or maker of a commodity or the contents of a pot, just as it could serve as a seal of quality or bestow a blessing.[25]
The high relief obverse of this cruciform stamp shows a mirror image of the inscription ΑΘΑΝΑΣΙΑ (*Athanasia*), which is the Ancient Greek word for 'immortality'. The reverse is furnished with a little grip. Such stamps were used to mark loaves of bread destined for ritual or religious purposes, such as the Christian Eucharist, but were also widely used in everyday life.[26] Invocations or blessings such as the one on this object suggest that it was intended for ritual purposes. Comparable stamps have been found in Egypt but were used all over the eastern Mediterranean. |CF|

HAND CROSS

Authors not documented • (Ethiopia) • Probably 19th cent. • Brass • 37 × 15.5 × 1 cm

Users, custodians before European appropriation not documented • Marianne Emrath • Sold in 2014 from Emrath's estate to Shimelis Lemma on behalf of (?) to the Staatliche Museen zu Berlin, Ethnologisches Museum, inv. no. III A 5709

Founded in the year 316, this Ethiopian church is the oldest in the world. The symbol of the cross is not immediately apparent on the object exhibited here, but is brought to the fore only by the play of light on the intricate ornamentation. The shape is reminiscent of the ancient Egyptian *ankh*, a symbol associated with immortality and life force. In Ethiopia, the cross is believed to protect believers against danger and disease. It is therefore regarded as a powerful talisman |see below|.[24] Such a cross is held by dignitaries with priestly functions during religious ceremonies such as processions and church services, but also at secular public ceremonies. It marks the holders out as members of the clerical caste and symbolises their high social rank |see bottom|. |TS|

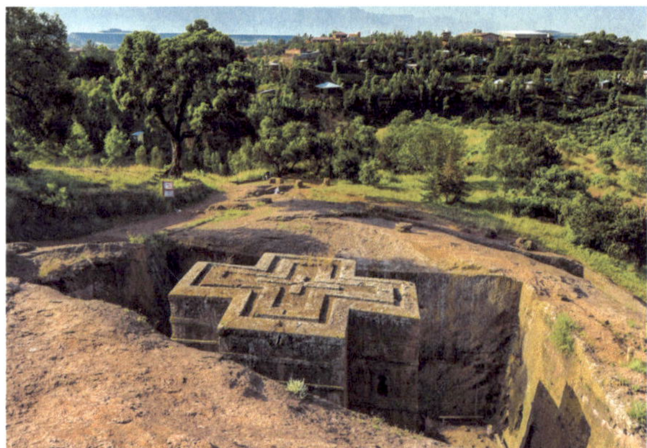

The cruciform Bet Giyorgis (House of Saint George) is one of the eleven monolithic churches in Lalibela, Ethiopia. This church complex was created in the 12th and 13th centuries as a symbol of Ethiopian Christians' strongly felt ties to the Holy Land.

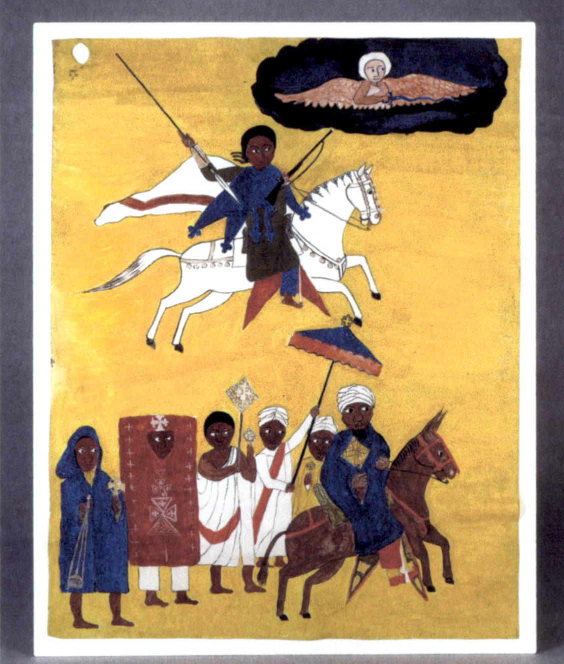

Procession of Ethiopian priests, paint on parchment, 79 × 65 cm
London, British Museum

Riding on a brown horse at the head of the procession is a priest in a blue vestment holding a golden hand cross in his right hand.

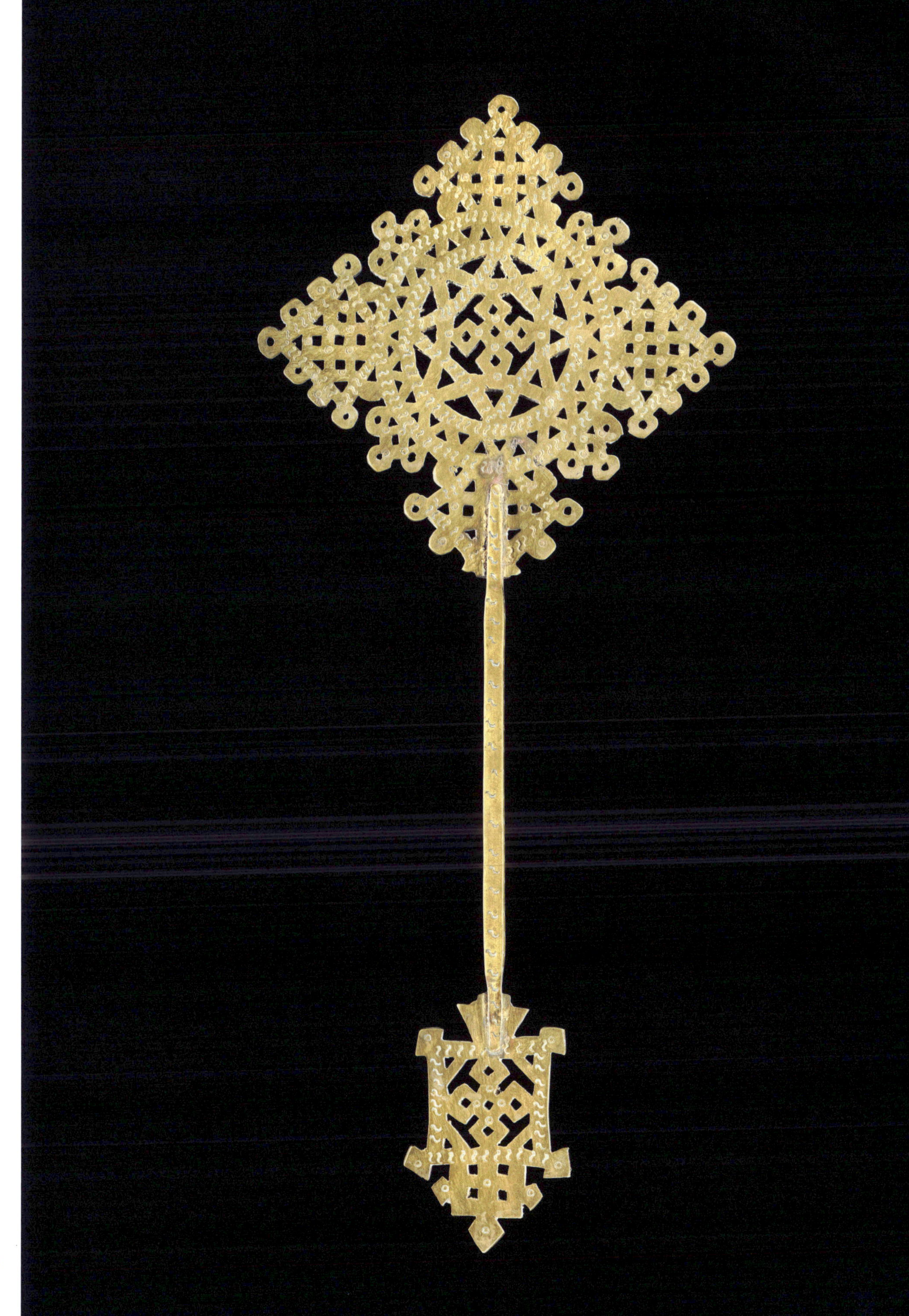

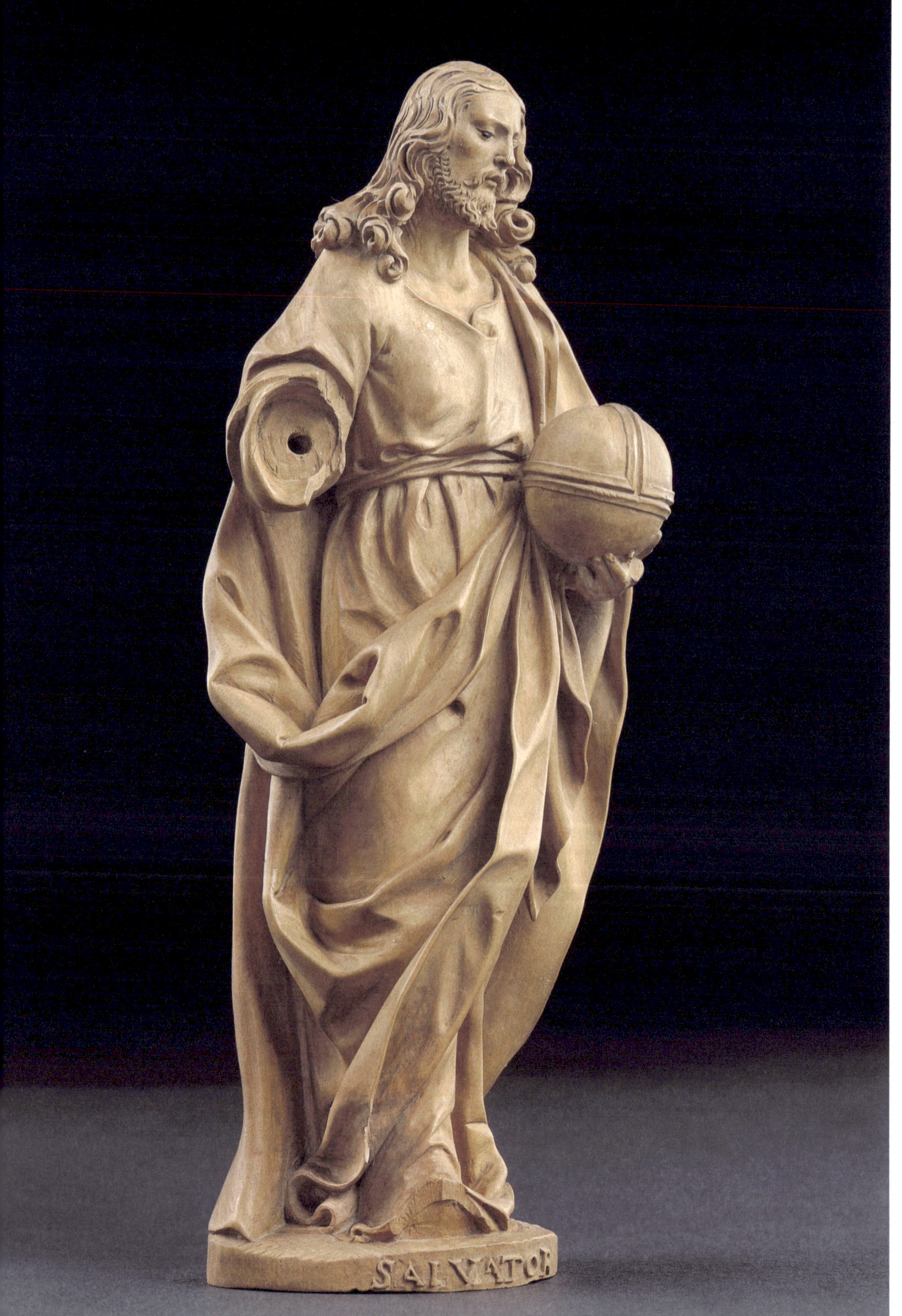
S.ALVATOR

CHRISTUS SALVATOR

Frans van Loo • Flanders (Belgium) • c. 1640 • boxwood • 16 × 6.6 × 4.4 cm (without the mount)

Possible previous owners unknown • Purchased in 1916, through the Munich art dealer Aaron Siegfried Drey, by the Kaiser-Friedrich-Museum, Berlin (today: Staatliche Museen zu Berlin, Skulpturensammlung und Museum für Byzantinische Kunst, inv. no. 7713) • No evidence of unjust acquisition is known of at this time.

Large-format depictions of Jesus and his Disciples, also known as 'Apostle Cycles', had adorned columns or pillars inside churches since the Middle Ages |see below|. Among the works inspired by them is this finely carved boxwood statuette of Christus Salvator wearing a long, belted robe and looking ponderously at the globe in his left hand. His missing right hand was probably raised in blessing over it. The inscription SALVATOR in raised majuscule on the plinth identifies him as the saviour of the world.

The disciples whom Jesus selected from among his numerous followers were called on to continue his work and to spread the Gospel. The figure would originally have been surrounded by the twelve apostles and formed a group with them. Its diminutive size suggests that van Loos's statuette, flanked by twelve others, originally stood on a household altar inside a private home. |HUK|

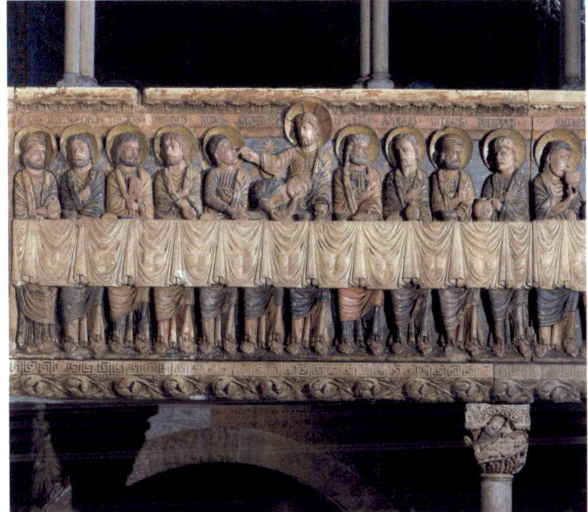

Detail of the rood screen separating the choir reserved for the monks from the nave. The carvings include a depiction of the Last Supper. Anselmo da Campione, Rood Screen: Last Supper, Modena Cathedral, Italy, 1160–1180, wood carving, polychromy

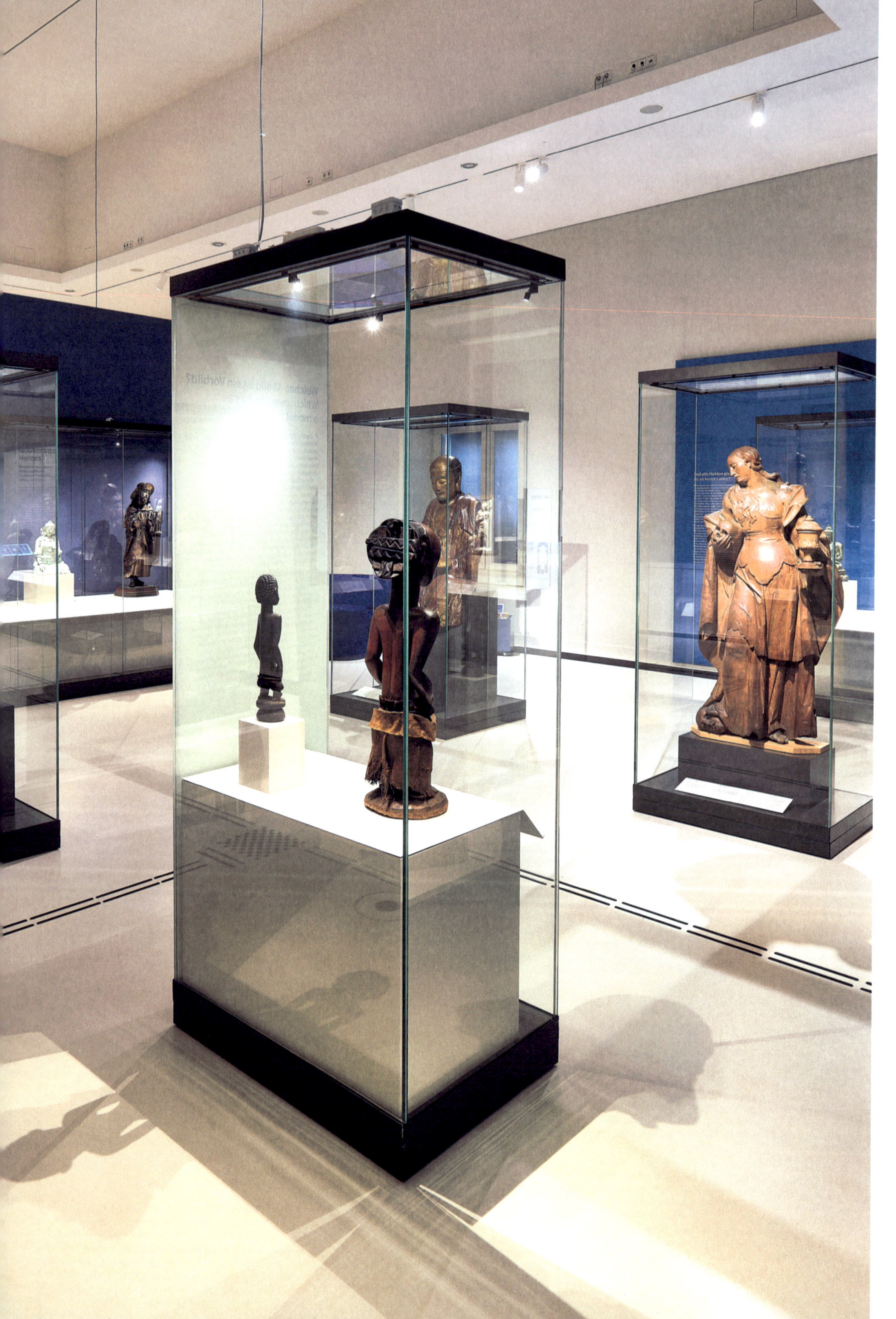

CHAPTER 5

WHICH IMAGE SERVES AS A MODEL?

The objects grouped together in this chapter alert us to the role of sculptures as vehicles of values and norms. None of the figures is a portrait in the sense of a true likeness of a particular individual. They rather represent fundamental social principles and convey values and character traits that the community considered worth aspiring to. In this sense they were iconic, as is apparent in their body language, facial expressions and how they wear their hair. These are the attributes that identify the figure from Europe as Mary Magdalene. The visualisation of an iconic figure in East Asia and Central Africa, by contrast, was not always tied to a particular individual. The pupils of the Buddha are depicted as representative of all Buddhist monks and their ascetic way of life. The two works from Central Africa stand for the social status of ancestors generally, but at the same time seem to be pointing to a specific ancestor or kinship relationship. |TS, BB|

SAINT MARY MAGDALENE

Johann Michael Düchert, attributed • Heidelberg (Germany) • 1750 • lime-wood • 155 × 73 × 36 cm

First known previous owner: Julius Böhler, c. 1900 an art dealer in Munich • Sold in 1921 to the Kaiser-Friedrich-Museum, Berlin (today: Staatliche Museen zu Berlin, Skulpturensammlung und Museum für Byzantinische Kunst, inv. no. 7989) • No evidence of unjust acquisition is known of at this time.

This standing figure of Mary Magdalene wears a long, elegant gown attesting to her past life as a courtesan. Her sorrowful face, her hair worn loosely down her back, and the jar of ointment in her right hand tell of the instant of her conversion. The Gospel of Saint Luke (Luke 7:36–50) relates how while Jesus was at supper one day, the sinner Mary Magdalene knelt before him and bathed his feet in her tears, wiped them dry with her long hair and then anointed them with a fragrant oil. Mary Magdalene joined Christ's disciples and was also present at his crucifixion and entombment. According to the Gospels (Mark 16:9 and John 20:14–18 for example), she was the one who first saw and recognised the risen Christ, though she was not allowed to touch him. Mary Magdalene thus embodies the hope of forgiveness and is an example of how devotion to God can cleanse sinners of their sins. In the early fifteenth century and throughout the sixteenth, the attribute of the pot of ointment was joined, or sometimes replaced, by a crucifix or death's head as a reminder of her love of Christ and of his sufferings.[1] |HUK|

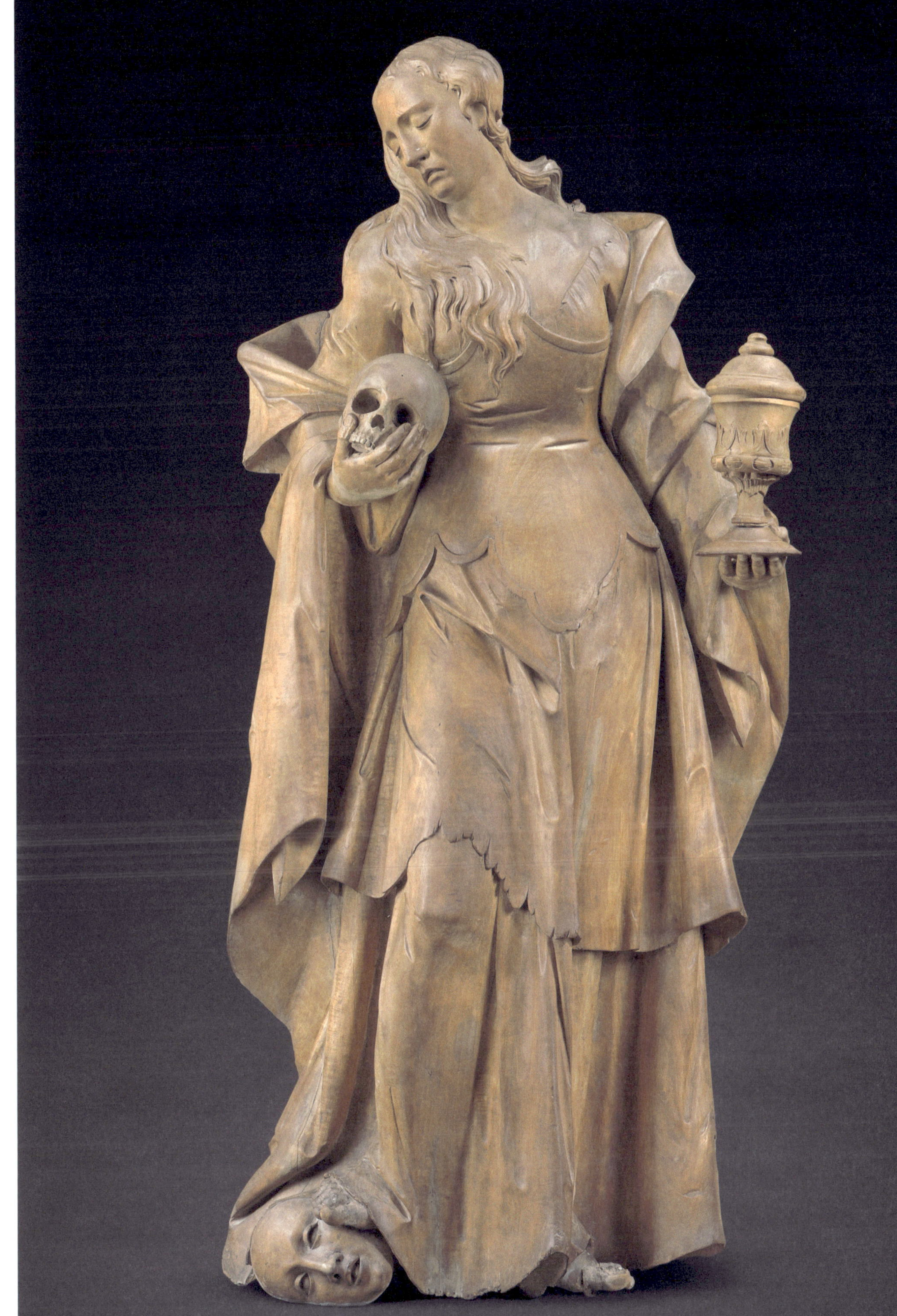

DISCIPLE OF THE BUDDHA (SANSKRIT: ARHAT)

Author not documented • (China) • Ming Dynasty (1368–1644) • wood, lacquered and painted, with gilding • 137 × 71.5 × 75 cm

First known previous owner: Paul Wegener, from 1906–1948 actor for the stage and screen in Berlin • Sold in 1958 from Wegener's estate to the Museum für Völkerkunde, Berlin (today: Staatliche Museen zu Berlin, Ethnologisches Museum, inv. no. I D 36837) • The object originates from a region that was partly under the influence of colonial powers from 1842 onwards. The possibility of unlawful acquisition cannot, therefore, be ruled out if it was put on the market after 1842.

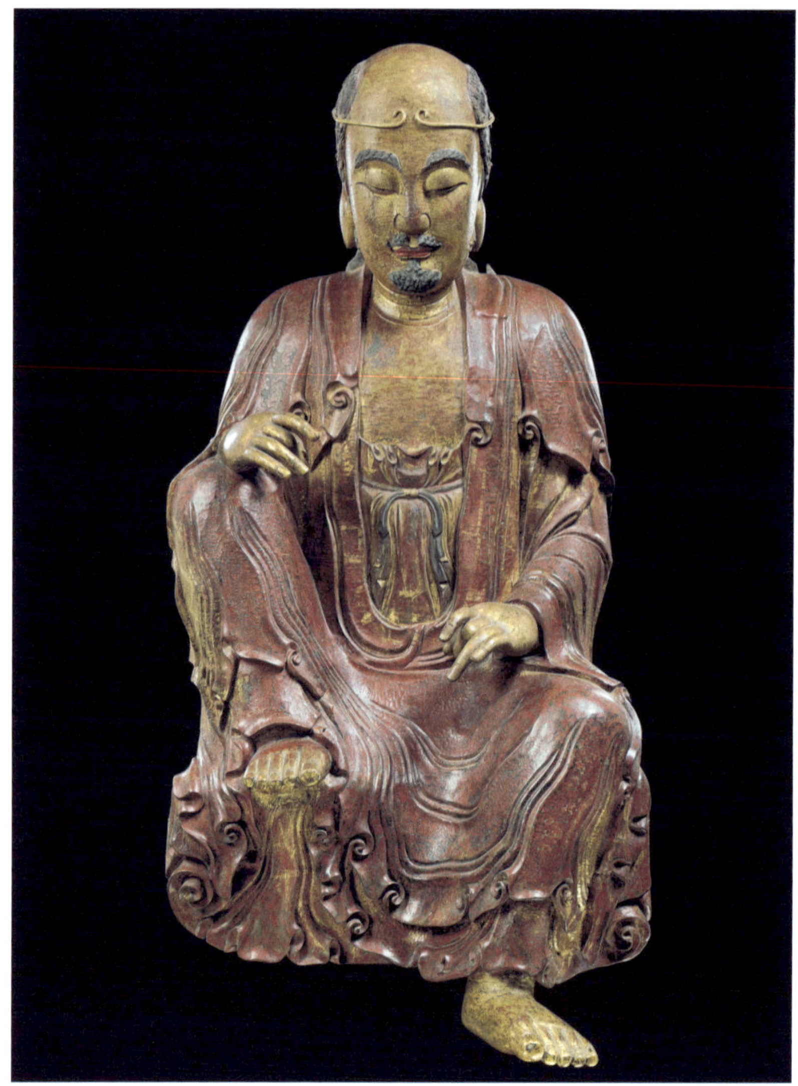

36

Starting in the seventh century, the Chinese venerated disciples of the historical Buddha as models of the ascetic way of life. Sculptures like this one were arranged in groups of sixteen, eighteen or even five hundred [see p. 75 bottom] without making any one of them identifiable. They are recognisable as the Buddha's disciples on account of their shaved heads and monk's garb. According to legend, the Buddha's disciples will linger on in the world, guarding the Buddha's teachings until the future Buddha Maitreya appears and a new age dawns.[2]

DISCIPLE OF THE BUDDHA (SANSKRIT: ARHAT)

Author not documented • (China) • Ming Dynasty (1368–1644) • wood, lacquered and painted, with gilding • 139 × 70 × 75 cm

First known previous owner: Paul Wegener, from 1906–1948 actor for the stage and screen in Berlin • Sold in 1958 from Wegener's estate to the Museum für Völkerkunde, Berlin (today: Staatliche Museen zu Berlin, Ethnologisches Museum, inv. no. I D 36838) • The object originates from a region that was partly under the influence of colonial powers from 1842 onwards. The possibility of unlawful acquisition cannot, therefore, be ruled out if it was put on the market after 1842.

37

The two wooden statues probably belonged to a larger group of disciples of the Buddha, which in China's Chan Buddhist temples would have had a dedicated room of their own. The seated figures' relaxed pose and contemplative facial expressions tell of their detachment from all social constraints. They also idealise the monastic way of life as the path to liberation,[3] and remind both monks and lay followers of Buddhism's origins. |BB|

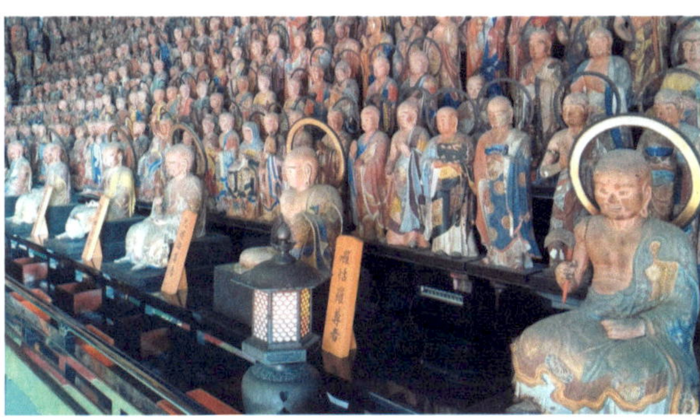

500-Arhat Hall of the Nakaya-madera, Takara-zuka, Hyōgo Province, Japan, photograph of 2019

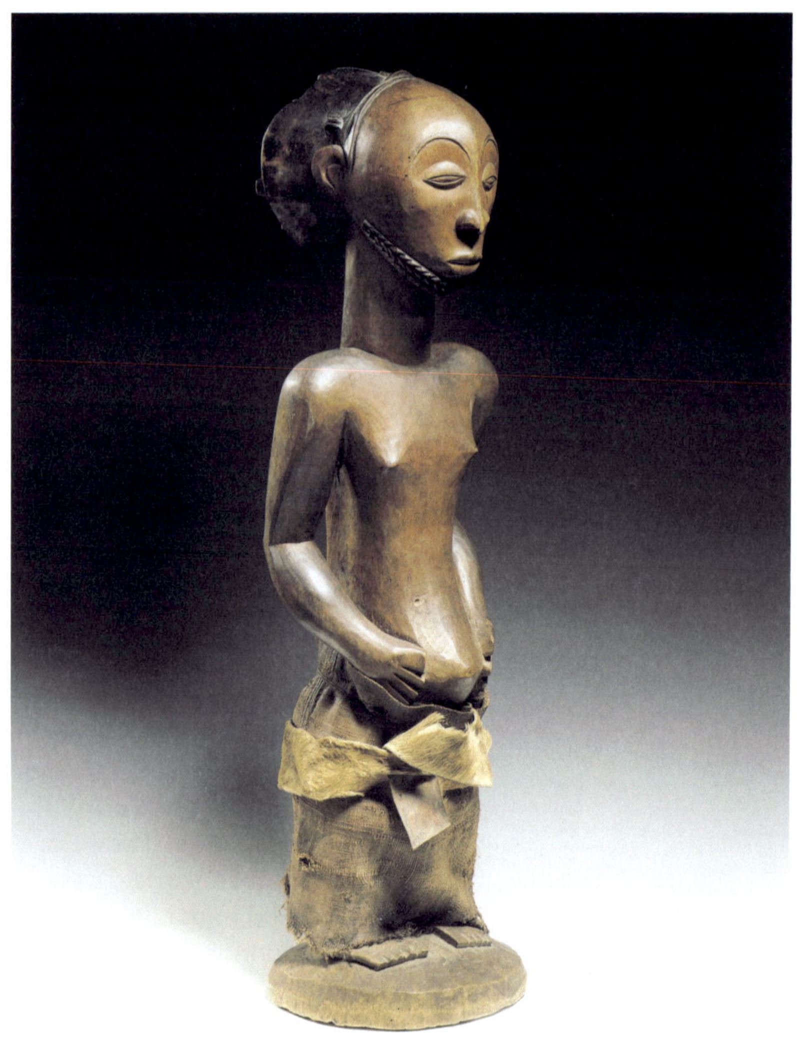

Authors not documented • Hemba region, Urua (DR Congo) • 19th cent. • wood, fur, raffia • 83 × 25 × 23.5 cm

Users, custodians before European appropriation not documented • Hans S. von Ramsay, from 1896–1898 chief colonial officer at the Ujiji station, Lake Tanganika • Sold in 1897 to the Königliches Museum für Völkerkunde, Berlin (today: Staatliche Museen zu Berlin, Ethnologisches Museum, inv. no. III E 5200 a–c) • The object originates from a region that at the time of its appropriation was under colonial rule. We regard colonialism as a context of systemic injustice. Thus even gifts and documented purchases cannot invariably be regarded as having been lawfully acquired.

This Hemba figure connected to a specific family and its history strengthened family cohesion by commemorating a high-ranking ancestor.[4] It is articulated in a visual idiom that was consolidated over a long period and translates the individual appearance of a person known by name into a very striking, idealised figure. The fine facial features, high domed brow and beard below the chin call to mind the features deemed necessary to a religious dignitary. The contemplative gaze, viewed in conjunction with the hands resting on the stomach, would have conveyed inviolability, strength and constancy.[5] The figure was not exhibited publicly, but rather kept in a mausoleum.[6] |TS|

FEMALE ANCESTOR FIGURE

Authors not documented • Tabwa region, village near Kalimba (DR Congo) • Late 19th cent. • wood, iron, plant fibres • 49 × 10.8 × 8.5 cm

Users, custodians before European appropriation not documented • Paul Reichard, from 1883–84 a participant (?) in the expedition from Urua to Katanga (DR Congo) initiated by Leopold II and funded in part by the Afrikanische Gesellschaft Berlin • Gifted in 1886 to the Königliches Museum für Völkerkunde, Berlin (today: Staatliche Museen zu Berlin, Ethnologisches Museum, inv. no. III E 1881) • The object was appropriated or acquired during the period of colonial conquest.

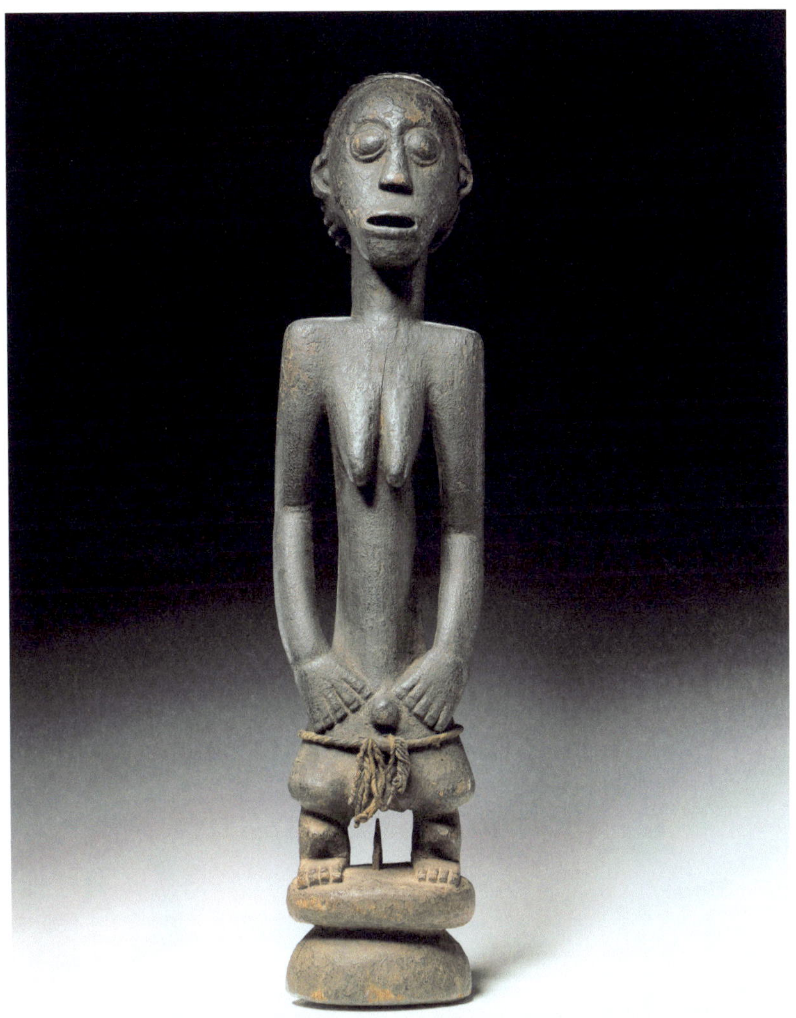

The presence of ancestors and their influence on their community's well-being play an important role in many African cultures. A vast array of visual works was created to facilitate communication with them and recall their exceptional deeds.[7] This Tabwa ancestor figure is remarkable for its symmetrical design. Her salient features are her elongated torso and strikingly modelled hair. Her hands resting on her flanks emphasise her navel and so forge a link to her own female ancestors.[8] This ancestor figure probably served as a reminder of shared ancestry as the origin and basis of cultural affiliation. The ornamental scars on the figure's back probably represent key crossroads in the Tabwa's long migration history. As cultural codes, they addressed the collective memory of the Tabwa as a knowledge community.[9] |TS|

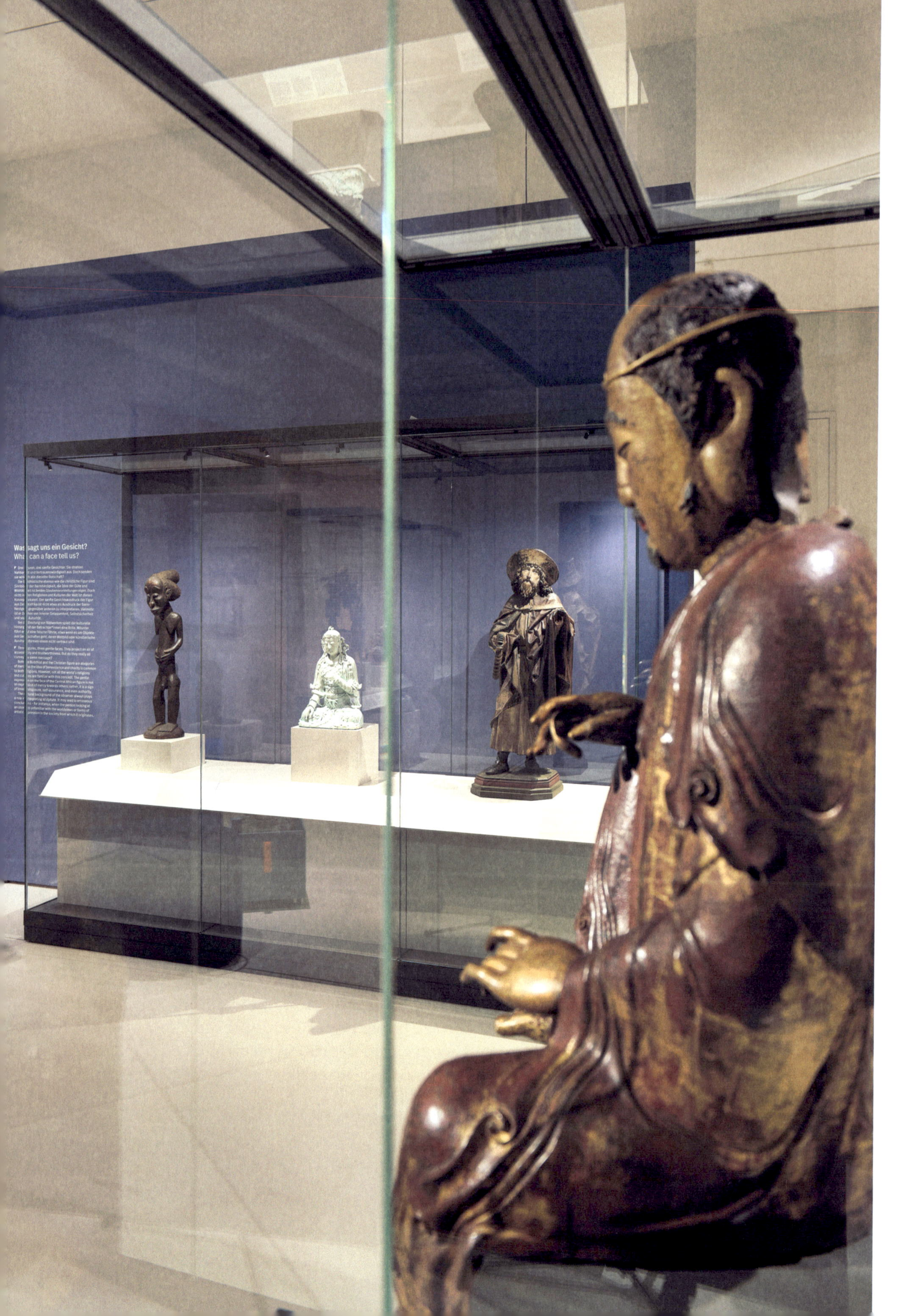

WHAT CAN A FACE TELL US?

The faces of the figures exhibited here seem well-meaning. They come across as exceptionally attentive, approachable and trustworthy. But does this mean that they all embody the same message? The Christian and Buddhist works shown here are thought to epitomise compassion, which is central to both religions. Yet such a concept cannot simply be transferred one to one to completely different societies and their visual works. The gentle facial expression of the ancestor figure from the Democratic Republic of Congo (cat. no. 41), for example, is less an expression of compassion for others than a sign of equanimity, self-confidence and authority. ⸺

Since our gaze is inevitably shaped by both individual and cultural factors, it can lead us to misinterpret objects from other cultures, whose views, attitudes and artistic forms of expression are not equally familiar to everyone. |TS, BB|⸺

Author not documented •
Chiemgau (Germany) •
c. 1500 • Pinewood
with later polychromy •
106 × 40 × 34 cm

First known previous owner:
James Simon, c. 1900 en-
trepreneur and patron of the
arts in Berlin • Gifted in
1918 to the Kaiser-Friedrich-
Museum, Berlin (today:
Staatliche Museen zu Berlin,
Skulpturensammlung und
Museum für Byzantinische
Kunst, inv. no. 8110) • No evi-
dence of unjust acquisition
is known of at this time.

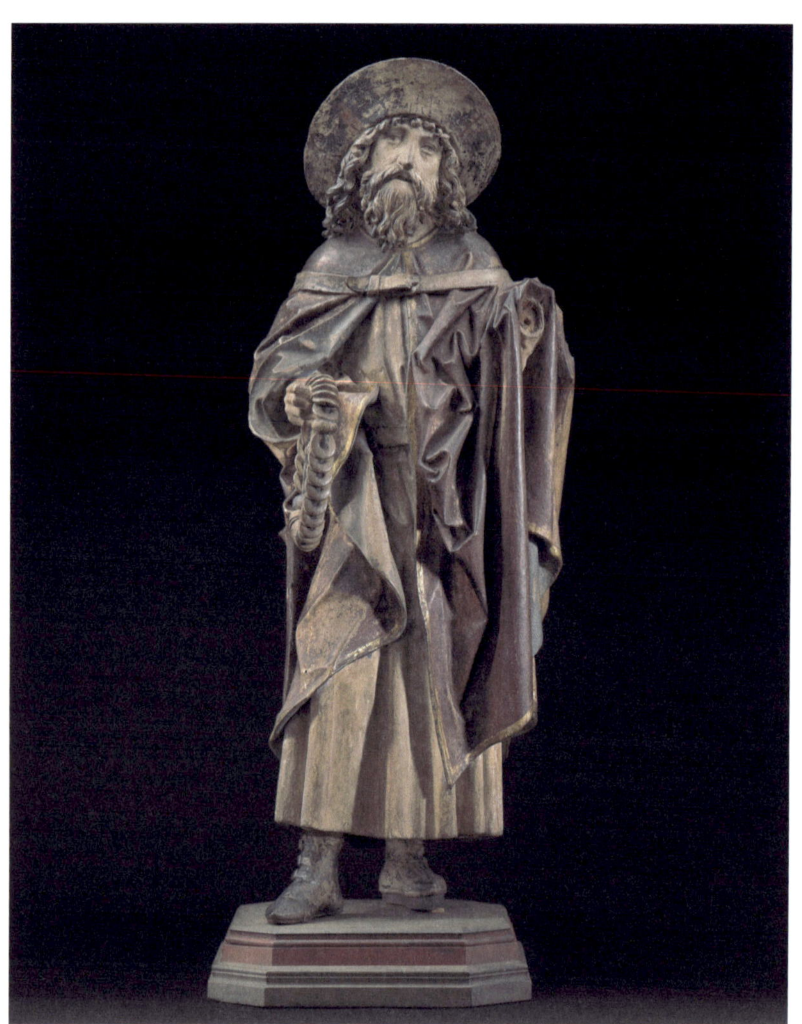

The tomb of the Apostle James in Compostela in north-western
Spain was an important shrine for medieval Christian pilgrims,
who flocked there from all over Western Europe, most of them
on foot. James has remained the patron saint of pilgrims to
this day and is depicted here as one of them, wearing buckled
shoes and a broad-brimmed hat, and with a knapsack on his
back.[1] In his left hand he would have held a pilgrim's staff. In
his right he holds a string of beads, also known as a rosary.
The rosary prayer (in fact five prayers with a total of fifty *Hail
Marys*, five *Our Fathers*, and five *Glory bes*) is the most wide-
spread form of Catholic devotion still practised today.
The societies of medieval Europe were steeped in the saints,
their legends, and the cults that grew up around them. As protective role models, they inspired interpretations of history and
prompted the creation of numerous images. Both people and
places were named after them.
Although clearly exhausted from his long journey, the figure
of Saint James looks very much alive. His gentle gaze is a reminder of the merciful, benevolent way in which the saint is
believed to watch over the faithful. |JC|

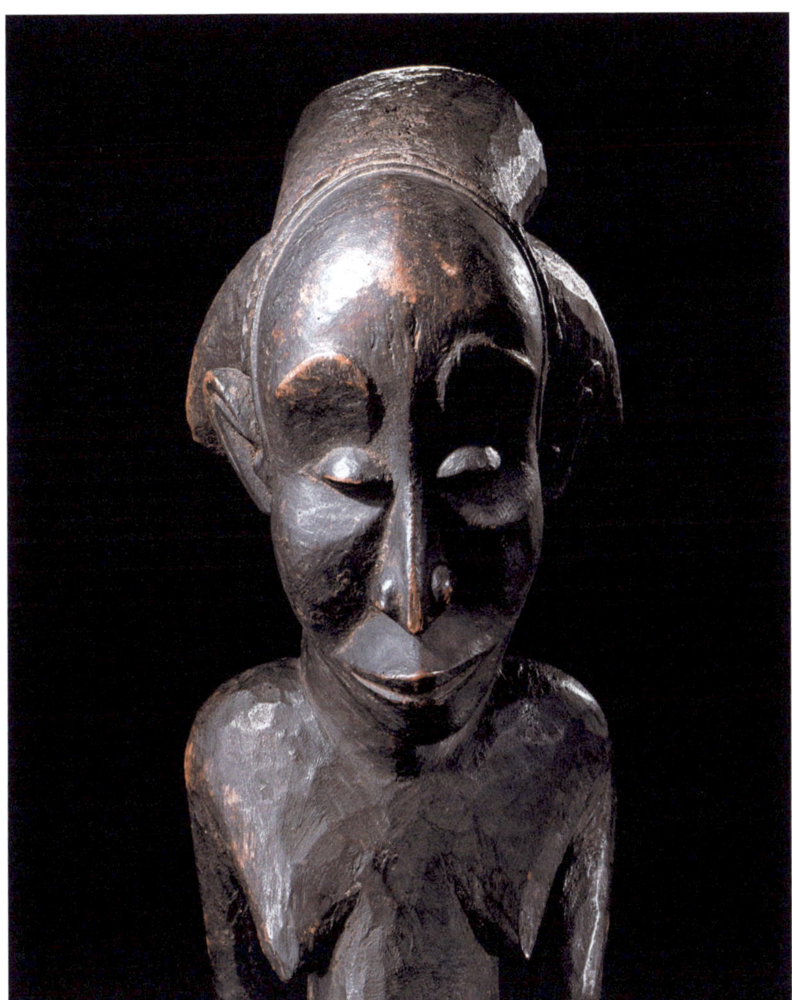

MALE ANCESTOR FIGURE

Workshop of the 'Bull Master' • Luba region (DR Congo) • 19th cent. • wood • 84 × 20 × 20 cm

Users, custodians before European appropriation not documented • Lieutenant-Colonel Göring • Sold in 1903 to the Königliches Museum für Völkerkunde, Berlin (today: Staatliche Museen zu Berlin, Ethnologisches Museum, inv. no. III C 16999) • The object comes from a region that at the time of its appropriation was under colonial rule. We regard colonialism as a context of systemic injustice. Thus even gifts and documented purchases cannot invariably be regarded as having been lawfully acquired.

41

At the time of its creation, this ancestor figure from the Luba region (Democratic Republic of Congo) embodied the ideal of an exemplary life as well as recalling the spiritual power of ancestors. The facial features of an aging man, the hands resting on the stomach and the upright pose present him as an experienced dignitary endowed with serenity and wisdom. In the belief system of the Luba, this striking figure probably served as a counterfoil to the timeless depiction of rulers as men of action. Perhaps what the figure conveys is an evolving understanding of leadership qualities. Western scholars take the view that this work was commissioned, and on grounds of its design have attributed it to the workshop of the 'Bull Master'.[2] |TS|

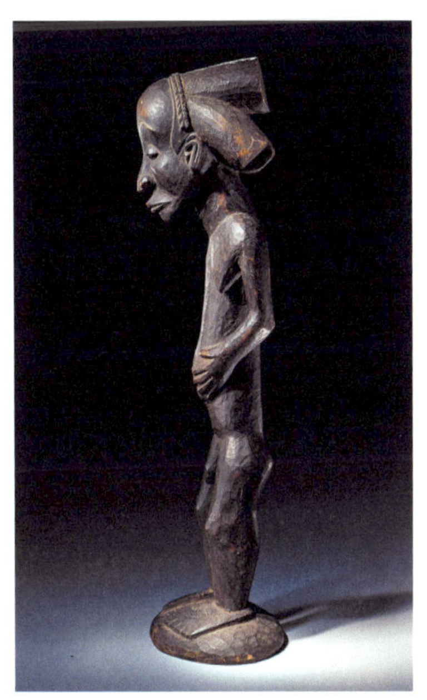

BODHISATTVA AVALOKITESHVARA

Authors unknown • Jingdezhen (China) • Yuan Dynasty (1279–1368) • porcelain with Qingbai glaze • 46.5 × 31 × 21 cm

First known previous owner: Eugen Pander, Professor of Economics in Beijing • Sold in 1890 to the Königliches Museum für Völkerkunde, Berlin (today: Staatliche Museen zu Berlin, Ethnologisches Museum, inv. no. I D 9811) • The object originates from a region that was partly under the influence of colonial powers from 1842 onwards. The possibility of unlawful acquisition cannot, therefore, be ruled out if it was put on the market after 1842.

With his princely adornments, this ***BODHISATTVA AVALOKITESHVARA*** embodies the selfless benevolence and empathy of the Buddha,[3] as expressed by the gentle smile playing on his lips. His legs crossed in the lotus position suggest that he is meditating, although his facial features make him seem eminently approachable.

The white glaze covering the figure probably had a ritual function and served as an aid to the imagination in secret Buddhist rituals. A ritual handbook from the Mongol period (1279–1368) describes step by step how practising Buddhists should imagine themselves as perfectly white, like the moon. This would enable them to identify with ***AVALOKITESHVARA***,[4] as whose embodiment they were empowered to open the gates of hell and release the dead from their torments. |BB|

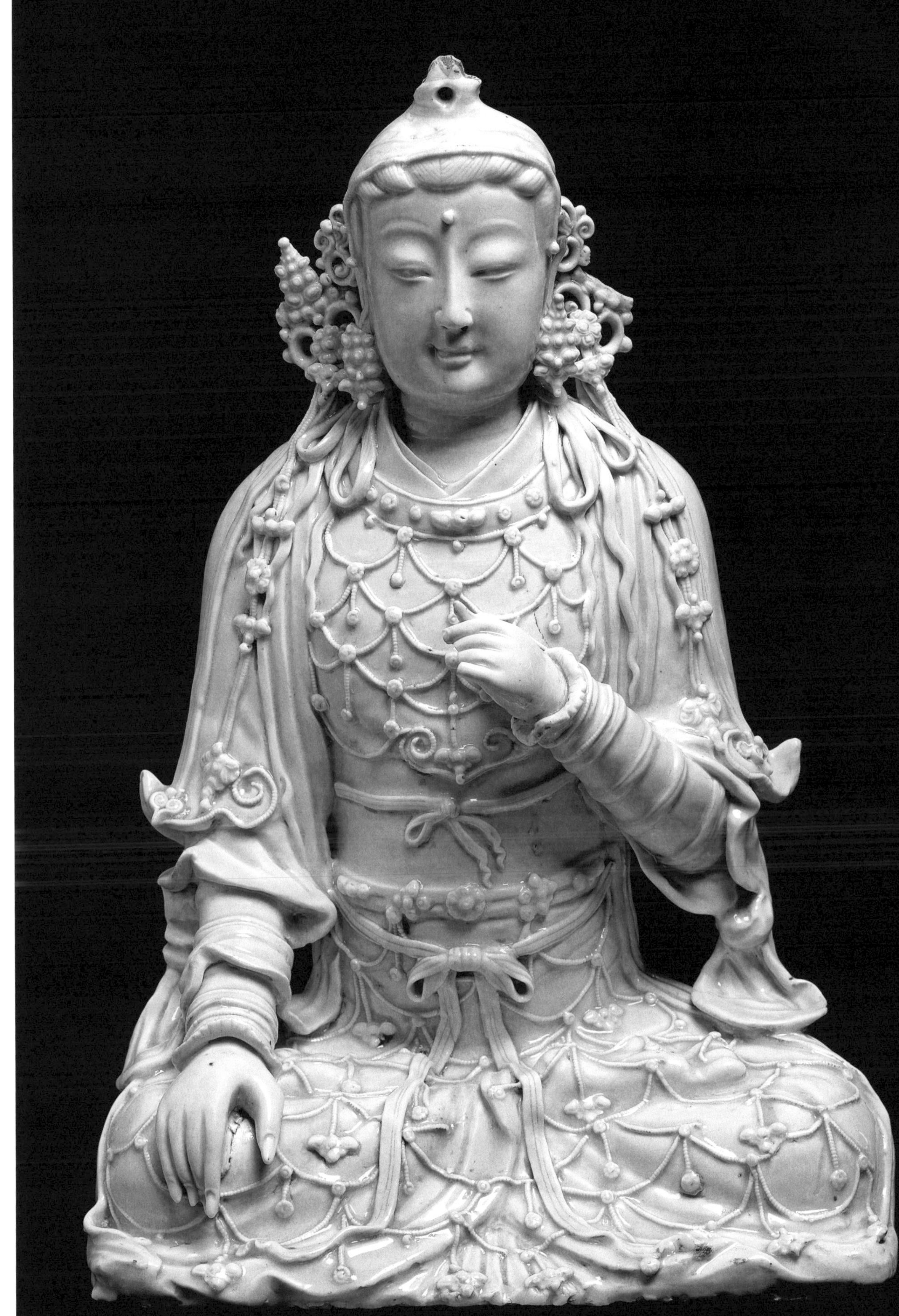

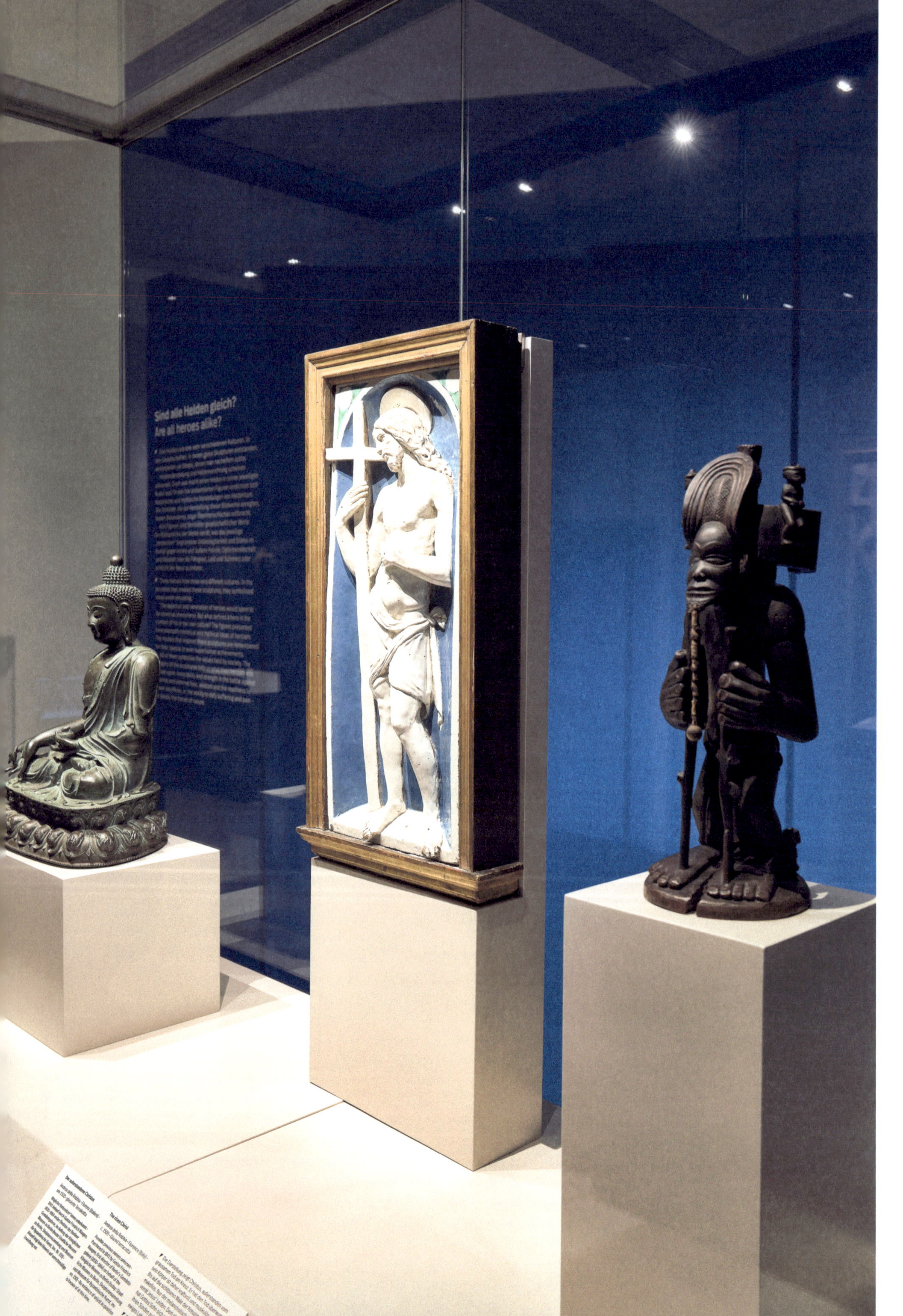

CHAPTER 7

ARE ALL HEROES ALIKE?

Here we have juxtaposed three central figures of identification: Chibinda Ilunga for the Chokwe in Angola and the Democratic Republic of Congo, Buddha for followers of the Buddhist schools, and Jesus Christ for Christians. All three purportedly performed superhuman feats and are regarded as heroes by their communities. ⸻

A comparison of these works as depictions of heroes reveals that the three cultures under discussion bring completely different criteria to bear when determining an individual's status as hero. Packed into the visual language of each of them, in other words, are concepts of both historical and mythical heroism. They therefore vary considerably from a man bursting with energy to a figure deep in meditation and a conqueror of pain and suffering. In this case, too, it is important to view the figures from more than just one angle and to remind ourselves that they fulfilled not just religious but also social and political functions. As figures of identification, all three sculptures embody social values. While both self-sacrifice and wisdom are manifested in the heroic depictions of Christ and Buddha, the aspect of Chibinda Ilunga that is foregrounded is his invincibility. |TS, BB| ⸻

THE RISEN CHRIST

Andrea della Robbia •
Florence (Italy) • c. 1500 •
glazed terracotta •
57 × 25 cm

Possible previous owners
unknown • Purchased in 1842
by Gustav Friedrich Waa-
gen, from 1830–1864 the
first director of the Berliner
Gemäldegalerie, on behalf
of the Königliche Museen
zu Berlin (today: Staatliche
Museen zu Berlin, Skulp-
turensammlung und Museum
für Byzantinische Kunst,
inv. no. 150) • No evidence of
unjust acquisition is known
of at this time.

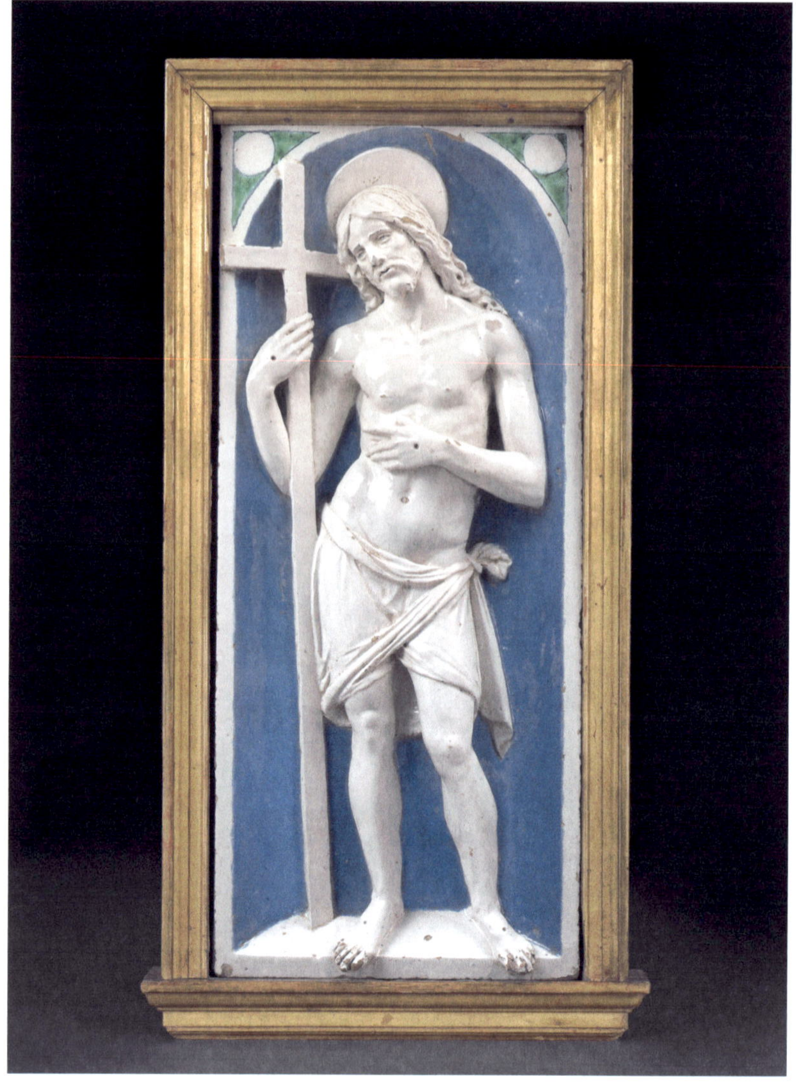

43

Christ stands before us clad only in a loincloth. In his right hand
he holds a cross, while with his left hand he points to a wound.
The holes in his hands and feet caused by his crucifixion are still
visible. He stands on a white surface that could be read either
as an altar table or as the floor of a niche. Here, Christ is presented as a vanquisher of death. Despite the cruelty of his
execution, his muscular body is unbroken and without blem-
ish – apart from the wounds in his hands, feet and side. His
melancholy expression tells of his sufferings. According to Christianity, Jesus was the Son of God who died on the cross to
atone for our sins and after three days rose again from the
dead. The faithful hope that through Christ's sacrifice they
will be accorded life eternal after death. The image of the risen
Christ was at once a focus of devotion and grounds for thanks-
giving and hope. |JC|

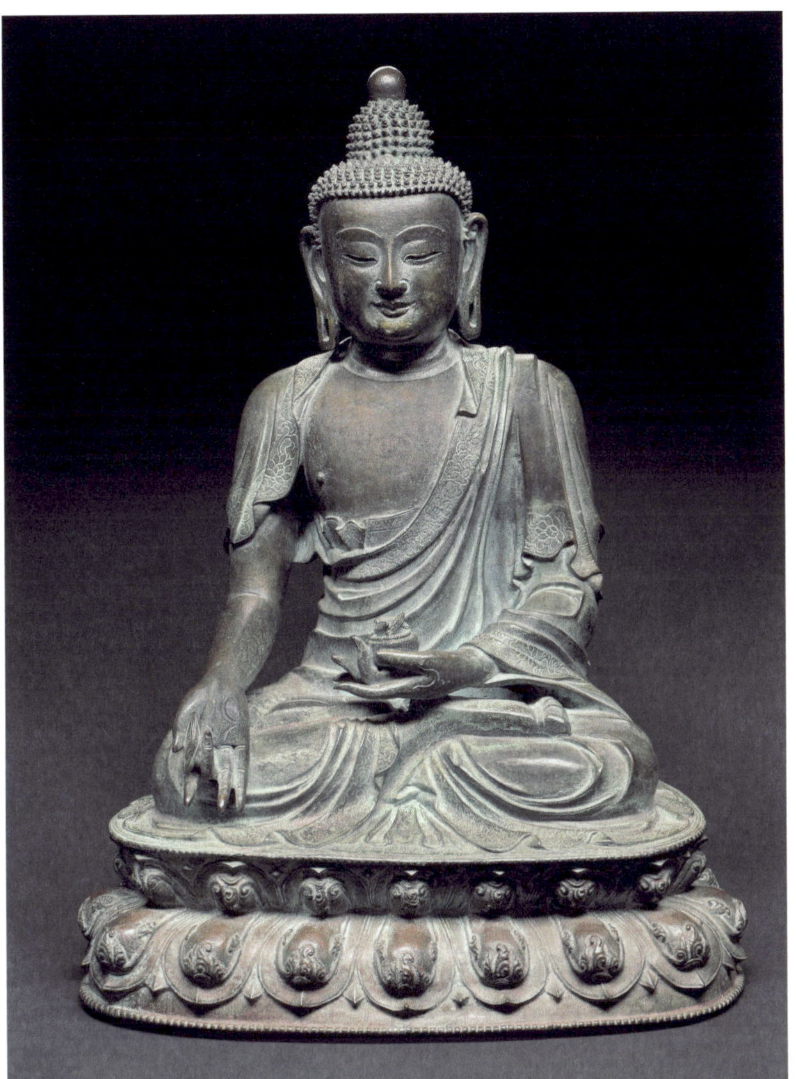

BUDDHA BHAISAJYAGURU

Author not documented • (China) • Ming Dynasty (1368–1644) • Mid-15th cent. • bronze • 46.5 × 34 × 25 cm

First known previous owner: Horst Golze • Sold in 1985 to the Museum für Völker-kunde, Berlin (today: Staatliche Museen zu Berlin, Ethnologisches Museum, inv. no. I D 46366) • No evidence of unjust acquisition is known of at this time.

Towards the end of his life, the historical Buddha Shakyamuni is said to have taken on the form of the 'medicine Buddha' *BHAISAJYAGURU*.[1] He embodies the healing aspects of Buddhahood, which released humans from the painful cycle of rebirth. Here he is shown meditating in the lotus position and with his right arm outstretched in the gesture of one granting a wish. He holds an Indian myrobalan fruit in his right hand, while the left hand lying in his lap cradles a spherical pot for preparing medicines. The nectar that it supposedly contains not only cures sickness but also grants longevity, prevents aging, and brings the dying back to life. |BB|

CHIBINDA ILUNGA

Authors not documented • Chokwe region (Angola) • 19th cent. • wood, cloth, hair, glass beads, plant fibres • 38.5 × 14.5 × 15.5 cm

Users, custodians before European appropriation not documented • Otto H. Schütt, cartographer, from 1877–1879 a participant(?) in Paul Gierow's expedition from Quimbundo to the lower Luachimo (Angola) in the service of the Afrikanische Gesellschaft Berlin • Sold in 1880 to the Königliches Museum für Völkerkunde, Berlin (today: Staatliche Museen zu Berlin, Ethnologisches Museum, inv. no. III C 1255) •

This compact sculpture shows Chibinda Ilunga, who is an important figure of identification for the Chokwe. It lends visible form to his royal heritage and spiritual potency. The erstwhile ruler is accompanied by three small spirits, under whose protection he founded the Kingdom of Lunda, or so the legend goes. His head covering and beard mark him out as a king, while his large hands and feet and forward-pointing arms symbolise strength and readiness for action. The numerous chiefs of the various Chokwe communities all appealed to this one hero and as active players in nineteenth-century trade used images like this one to reinforce their territorial claims in what is now Angola.[2] |TS|

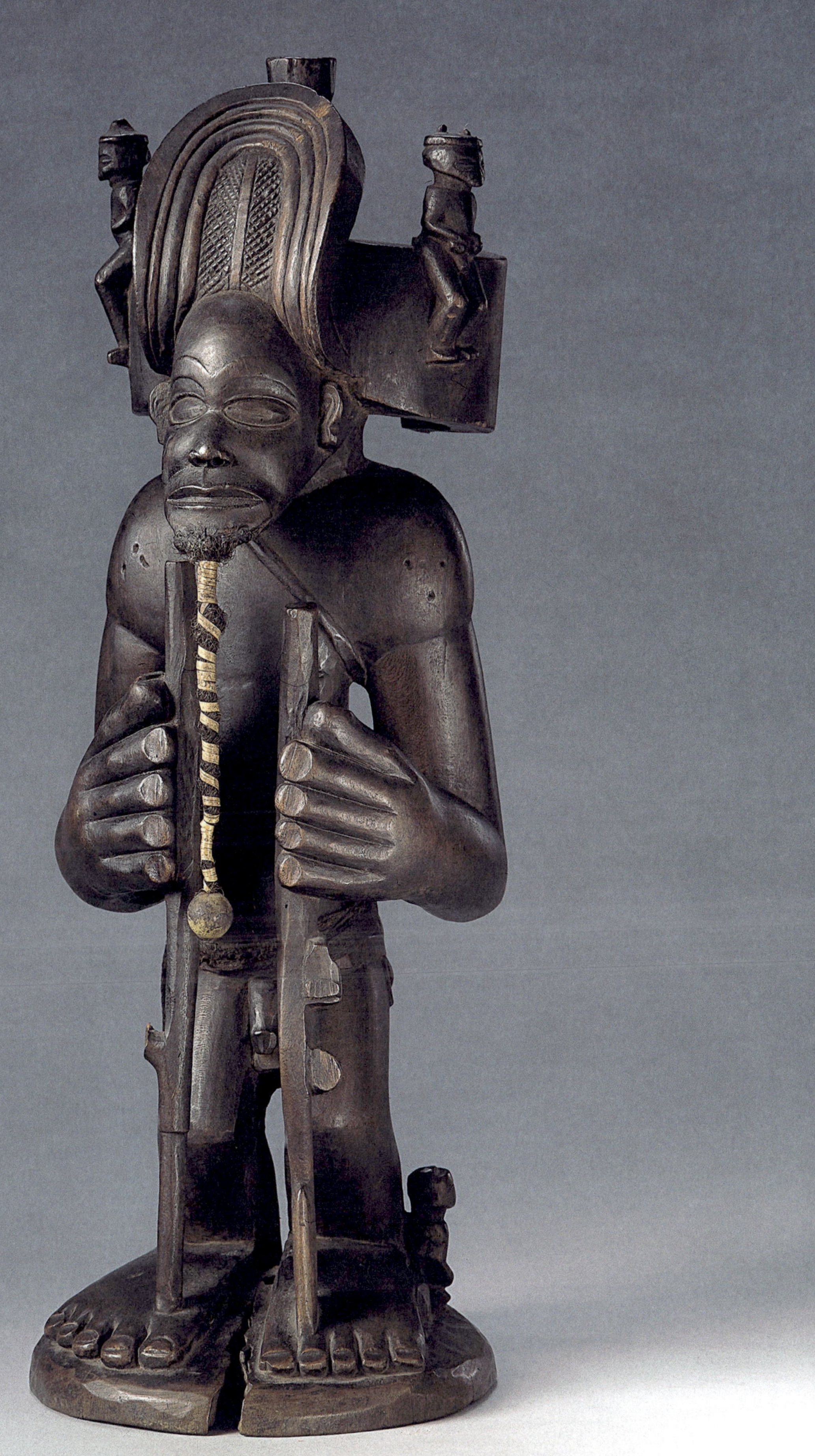

ANNOTATIONS

CHAPTER 1: *WHAT DOES PROTECTION MEAN HERE?*

1 Marinus W. de Visser, ' Die Pfauenkönigin (K'ung-tsioh ming-wang, Kujaki myo-o) in China und Japan', *Ostasiatische Zeitschrift*, 8 (1919): 370–87.

2 Heather Karmay, *Early Sino-Tibetan Art* (Warminster, 1975).

3 *Congo: Power and Majesty*, exh. cat. The Metropolitan Museum of Art, New York, ed. Alisa LaGamma (New Haven/London, 2015), pp. 221–62, esp. 221–22.

4 Wyatt MacGaffey, 'Minkisi on the Loango Coast', in *Minkisi: Skulpturen vom unteren Kongo*, exh. cat. Grassi-Museum für Völkerkunde zu Leipzig, Leipzig, ed. Claus Deimel (Berlin, 2012), pp. 27–33, esp. p. 33.

5 On the iconography of the Immaculata, see Louis Réau, *Iconographie de l'art chrétien* 2, no. 2 (1957–58); 75–83; see also Wolfgang Braunfels, *Lexikon der christlichen Ikonographie*, vol. 2 (Rome/Freiburg/Basel/Vienna, [1974] 1994), cols. 338–44, esp. 340–43.

6 Sabine Poeschel, *Handbuch der Ikonographie: Sakrale und profane Themen der bildenden Kunst* (Darmstadt, 2007), p. 119.

7 Réau, *Iconographie de l'art chrétien* (see note 2): 65.

CHAPTER 2: *HOW TO KEEP EVIL FORCES IN CHECK?*

1 *Ancestral Art of Gabon: From the Collections of the Barbier-Mueller Museum*, exh. cat. Dallas, Dallas Museum of Art, ed. Louis Perrois (Geneva, 1986), pp. 150–51; see also *African Art in the Cycle of Life*, exh. cat. Washington, DC, National Museum of African Art, ed. Roy Sieber and Roslyn A. Walker (Washington, DC, 1987), p. 80.

2 *Eternal Ancestors: The Art of the Central African Reliquary*, exh. cat. The Metropolitan Museum of Art, New York, ed. Alisa LaGamma and Barbara Drake Boehm (New Haven/New York, 2007), p. 300; *Kunst aus Afrika: Plastik, Performance, Design*, exh. cat. Berlin, Ethnologisches Museum, Staatliche Museen zu Berlin, ed. Peter Junge and Paola Ivanov (Berlin, 2005), p. 128.

3 Perrois, *Ancestral Art of Gabon* (see note 1), p. 150.

4 Réne de Nebesky-Wojkowitz, *Oracles and Demons of Tibet: The Cult and Iconography of the Tibetan Protective Deities* (The Hague, 1956).

5 Thomas Marcotty, *Dagger Blessing: The Tibetan Phurpa Cult: Reflections and Materials* (Delhi, 2017).

6 Louis Réau, *Iconographie de l'art chrétien* 3, no. 2 (1957–58): 570–71.

CHAPTER 3: *ARE THEY ALL REAL?*

1 *African Art in the Cycle of Life*, exh. cat. National Museum of African Art, Washington DC, ed. Roy Sieber and Roslyn A. Walker (Washington, DC, 1987), p. 139.

2 Louis Réau, *Iconographie de l'art chrétien* 2, no. 2 (1957–58), pp. 391–92.

3 Réau, ibid., pp. 948–50; see also Janette Witt, *Werke der Alltagskultur: Menasampullen*, Staatliche Museen zu Berlin – Preußischer Kulturbesitz – Skulpturensammlung und Museum für Byzantinische Kunst, Bestandskataloge, vol. 2, no. 1 (Wiesbaden, 2000), pp. 16–17.

4 Ibid., pp. 13–15.

5 This is proven by an inscription found in the ruins of a church in Haidar Pasha, not far from Kadıköy. See also Louis Duchesne, 'Inscription chrétienne de Bithynie', Bulletin de correspondance hellénique, vol. II (1878): 289–99; Carl Maria Kaufmann, *Handbuch der altchristlichen Epigraphik* (Freiburg, 1917), pp. 391–92.

6 Heino Kottkamp, *Der Stupa als Repräsentation des buddhistischen Heilsweges: Untersuchung zur Entstehung und Entwicklung architektonischer Symbolik* (Wiesbaden, 1992).

7 Yael Bentor, *Consecration of Images and Stupas in Indo-Tibetan Tantric Buddhism* (Leiden/New York/Cologne, 1996).

8 Miranda Eberle Shaw, *Buddhist Goddesses of India* (Princeton, 2006), pp. 291–305.

9 Yael Bentor, 'The Content of Stupas and Images and the Indo-Tibetan Concept of Relics', *The Tibet Journal*, 28 (2003): 21–48.

10 *Ancestral Art of Gabon: From the Collections of the Barbier-Mueller Museum*, exh. cat. Dallas Museum of Art, ed. Louis Perrois (Geneva, 1986), p. 45; see also Sieber and Walker, *African Art in the Cycle of Life* (see note 1), p. 138.

11 Kairn Klieman, 'Of Ancestors and Earth Spirits: New Approaches for Interpreting Central African Politics, Religion, and Art', in *Eternal Ancestors: The Art of the Central African Reliquary*, ed. Alisa LaGamma and Barbara Drake Boehm (New Haven/New York, 2007), p. 57.

12 Denise Patry Leidy, 'Asian Reliquaries', in LaGamma, *Eternal Ancestors*, p. 27.

CHAPTER 4: *CAN WORDS DESCRIBE THINGS?*

1 The term is derived from the museum's own system of classification. In the regional context such figures are called *minkisi*, which is also the word for the force that animates them.

2 On the functional context of this figure, see *Minkisi: Skulpturen vom unteren Kongo*, exh. cat. Leipzig, Grassi-Museum für Völkerkunde zu Leipzig, ed. Claus Deimel (Berlin, 2012).

3 On the sex of *nganga*, who could be either male or female, see Wyatt MacGaffey, *Art and Healing of the Bakongo Commented by Themselves: Minkisi from the Laman Collection* (Stockholm, 1991), p. 50.

4 On the translation of regional terms, see MacGaffey, ibid.

5 *Kunst aus Afrika: Plastik, Performance, Design*, exh. cat. Ethnologisches Museum, Staatliche Museen zu Berlin, Berlin, ed. Peter Junge and Paola Ivanov (Berlin, 2005), p. 117.

6 *African Art in the Cycle of Life*, exh. cat. National Museum of African Art, Washington DC, ed. Roy Sieber and Roslyn A. Walker (Washington, DC, 1987), p. 83. On the representation of still more functions, see Wyatt MacGaffey, 'Minkisi on the Loango Coast', in *Minkisi: Skulpturen vom unteren Kongo*, exh. cat. Grassi-Museum für Völkerkunde zu Leipzig, Leipzig, ed. Claus Deimel (Berlin, 2012), pp. 27–33, esp. pp. 31–32.

7 This is based on an entry in the main catalogue of the Ethnologisches Museum.

8 Object nos. III C 8104 b and III C 8104 c come with the following note: 'Kills anyone on demand and for payment. To obtain a reprieve, the condemned must pay to pull a nail out of a basket. For further details see note.'

9 For a detailed description of the materials and the aesthetic quality of the figure in relation to its functional context, see Junge and Ivanov 2005, p. 112.

10 Ibid., p. 114.

11 MacGaffey, 'Minkisi on the Loango Coast', in Deimel, *Minski* (see note 6), p. 30.

12 Réne de Nebesky-Wojkowitz, *Oracles and Demons of Tibet: The Cult and Iconography of the Tibetan Protective Deities* (The Hague, 1956).

13 Louise Tythacott and Chiara Bellini, 'Deity and Display: Meanings, Transformations, and Exhibitions of Tibetan Buddhist Objects', *Religions*, 11.6 (2020), https://doi.org/10.3390/rel11030106.

14 Louis Frédéric, *Buddhism. Flammarion Iconographic Guides* (Paris, 1995), pp. 144–45.

15 David L. Snellgrove, *Indo-Tibetan Buddhism: Indian Buddhists and Their Tibetan Successors* (London, 1987), p. 195.

16 David Quinter, *From Outcasts to Emperors: Shingon Ritsu and the Manjusri Cult in Medieval Japan* (Leiden, 2015).

17 Zhiru Ng, *The Making of a Savior Bodhisattva: Dizang in Medieval China* (Honolulu, 2007); see also Marinus W. de Visser, *The Bodhisattva Ti-Tsang (Jizo) in China and Japan* (Berlin, 1914).

18 Denise Patry Leidy, *The Art of Buddhism: An Introduction to its History and Meaning* (Boston, 2008), pp. 281–82.

19 As an example of this, see the following passage on the crucifixion from the very popular and influential fourteenth-century Meditationes de vita Christi: 'And you, if you have with fixed attention gazed upon your Lord, can tell how, from the sole of the Foot, even to His Head, there is no soundness in Him, there is no member, no sense, which has not endured some great pain or injury. Here, then, you have, indeed, enough on the Crucifixion and Death of our Lord, which happened at the sixth and ninth hours … But strive devoutly, faithfully, to give yourself to meditate upon this.' Cardinal Saint Bonaventure, *The Life of Christ*, trans. W. H. Hutchings (London, 1888), chap. 79, p. 272.

20 On the blending of the European and Congolese language of forms, see Walker and Sieber 1987, p. 124.

21 Ibid.

22 Louis Réau, *Iconographie de l'art chrétien 2*, no. 2 (1957–58): 7.

23 Ibid., 40–41.

24 Stanisław Chojnacki and Carolyn Gossage, *Ethiopian Crosses: A Cultural History and Chronology* (Milan, 2006).

25 Michael Grünbart and Susanne Lochner-Metaxas, 'Stempel(n) in Byzanz', in *Wiener Byzantinistik und Neogräzistik: Beiträge zum Symposion 40 Jahre Institut für Byzantinistik und Neogräzistik der Universität Wien im Gedenken an Herbert Hunger*, ed. Wolfgang Hörandner, Johannes Koder and Maria A. Stassinopoulou (Vienna, 2004), pp. 177–89.

26 *Die Welt von Byzanz – Europas östliches Erbe, Glanz, Krisen und Fortleben einer tausendjährigen Kultur*, exh. cat. Museum für Vor- und Frühgeschichte München, Munich, ed. Ludwig Wamser (Stuttgart, 2004), p. 341.

CHAPTER 5: *WHICH IMAGE SERVES AS A MODEL?*

1 Wolfgang Braunfels, *Lexikon der christlichen Ikonographie*, vol. 7 (Rome/Freiburg/Basel/Vienna, [1974 1994], col. 524.

2 Marinus W. de Visser, *The Arhats in China and Japan* (Berlin, 1923).

3 On the iconography of the Buddha pupils, see Eileen Hsiang-Ling Hsu, *Monks in Glaze: Patronage, Kiln Origin, and Iconography of the Yixian Luohans* (Leiden/Boston, 2017), p. 114.

4 *Heroic Africans: Legendary Leaders, Iconic Sculptures*, exh. cat. The Metropolitan Museum of Art, New York, ed. Alisa LaGamma (New Haven/London, 2011), pp. 225–26.

5 For a detailed description of the iconographic features of the Hemba ancestor figure, see LaGamma, ibid., pp. 230–32, 234.

6 Ibid., p. 228.

7 Elias K. Bongmba, 'Ancestor Veneration in Central Africa', in *Eternal Ancestors: The Art of the Central African Reliquary*, ed. Alisa LaGamma and Barbara Drake Boehm (New Haven/New York, 2007), pp. 79–85.

8 *Kunst aus Afrika: Plastik, Performance, Design*, exh. cat. Ethnologisches Museum, Staatliche Museen zu Berlin, ed. Peter Junge and Paola Ivanov (Berlin, 2005), p. 100.

9 *Tabwa: The Rising of a New Moon. A Century of Tabwa Art*, exh. cat. University of Michigan Museum of Art, Ann Arbor, MI, ed. Evan M. Maurer and Allen Roberts (Ann Arbor, MI, 1985).

CHAPTER 6: *WHAT CAN A FACE TELL US?*

1 Louis Réau, *Iconographie de l'art chrétien 3*, no 2 (1957–58): 693–95.

2 See also *Heroic Africans: Legendary Leaders, Iconic Sculptures*, exh. cat. The Metropolitan Museum of Art, New York, ed. Alisa LaGamma (New Haven/London, 2011), pp. 260–63.

3 Chün-fang Yü, Kuan-Yin: *The Chinese Transformation of Avalokiteśvara* (New York, 2001).

4 Chün-fang Yü and Chongxin Yao, 'Guanyin and Dizang: The Creation of a Chinese Buddhist Pantheon', *Asiatische Studien – Études asiatiques 70*, no. 3 (YEAR): 757–96, esp. 786.

CHAPTER 7: *ARE ALL HEROES ALIKE?*

1 Dorje Gyurme, 'The Buddhas of Medicine', in *Bodies in Balance: The Art of Tibetan Medicine*, ed. Theresia Hofer (Washington, DC, 2014), pp. 128–53, esp. p. 140.

2 *Heroic Africans: Legendary Leaders, Iconic Sculptures*, exh. cat. The Metropolitan Museum of Art, New York, ed. Alisa LaGamma (New Haven/London, 2011), pp. 183–88.

Bernadette Bröskamp (BB) studied Oriental Art History, Sinology and Comparative Religious Studies in Bonn, specialising in the Buddhist art of Tibet and China. She was on the team of the 2007 exhibition Tibet Monasteries Open Their Treasure Chambers in Berlin and has published numerous scholarly articles on Buddhist art. She has done research at the Lumbini International Research Institute in Nepal, has taught at universities in Bonn, Bochum and Berlin (FU), and has catalogued public and private collections of Tibetan and Mongolian art in Barcelona, Hong Kong and Switzerland.

Julien Chapuis (JC) has been Deputy Director of the Skulpturensammlung und Museum für Byzantinische Kunst, Staatliche Museen zu Berlin, at the Bode-Museum since 2008. From 1997 to 2007 he was a curator at The Cloisters, the medieval branch of the Metropolitan Museum of Art in New York. He has curated exhibitions and prepared publications on late-medieval painting and sculpture and on the history of the Berlin museums. He is currently working on an initiative to strengthen museums' education and outreach activities.

Hartmut Dorgerloh (HD) has been General Director and Chairman of the Board of the Stiftung Humboldt Forum Foundation im Berliner Schloss since 2018. From 2002 to 2018 he was General Director of the Stiftung Preussische Schlösser und Gärten Berlin-Brandenburg. The art historian and cultural manager has also been lecturing as an honorary professor at the Humboldt University of Berlin since 2004.

Cäcilia Fluck (CF) studied Coptology, Christian Archaeology and Egyptology at the universities of Münster and Leuven. She is a co-founder of the international study group "Textiles from the Nile Valley" and has been a research associate at the Museum für Byzantinische Kunst der Staatlichen Museen zu Berlin since 2010. Her research focus is on the late antique and early Christian art of Egypt, especially textiles.

Lars-Christian Koch (LCK) has been Director of the Collections of the Staatliche Museen zu Berlin im Humboldt Forum and hence Director of the Ethnologisches Museum und des Museums für Asiatische Kunst – Staatliche Museen zu Berlin since 2018.

Nathalie Küchen (NK) works as a project manager for exhibitions by the Stiftung Humboldt Forum im Berliner Schloss. After studying Art History, Cultural Studies and Political Science in Leipzig, Barcelona and Berlin, she worked on various projects for the KW Institute for Contemporary Art, the Haus der Kulturen der Welt and Kulturprojekten Berlin. In 2014 she co-curated Vanitas – Nothing Is Eternal Anyway, an exhibition at the Georg Kolbe Museum, Berlin, featuring works by artists such as Mona Hatoum, Dieter Roth and Tomás Saraceno.

Henriette Lavaulx-Vrécourt (HLV) works as a curator in the department of East and North Asia at the Ethnologisches Museum der Staatlichen Museen zu Berlin. Her most recent works are: "Erschließen von Museumsbeständen in Koproduktion mit indigenen Gemeinschaften" (2022), "Spuren des 'Boxerkrieges' in deutschen Museumssammlungen – eine gemeinsame Annäherung" (2022), "Berliner Schlachtenkupfer– 34 Druckplatten der Kaiser von China" (2021) and "Buddhismus auf dem Dach der Welt–Kunst und rituelle Objekte vom tibetischen Plateau" (2021).

Barbara Lenz (BL) studied Ethnology and Cultural Studies in Leipzig, Berlin and Leiden, was a research intern at the Ethnologisches Museum der Staatlichen Museen zu Berlin, and worked on a freelance basis in cultural education, focusing on the education and outreach activities of the Berlin museums. She has been curator for education and outreach at the Stiftung Humboldt Forum since 2018.

Tanja-Bianca Schmidt (TS) studied Art History in a global context, focusing on the African continent. Her principal lines of inquiry are critiques of power, difference theory, black identity and discrimination-sensitive approaches to art and film studies. She works as a political educator for various museums in Berlin and organises regular workshops on racially sensitive art history methods. She is currently a doctoral candidate in the project "Bildproteste in den Sozialen Medien", a project sponsored by the German Research Council at the Technical University of Dresden.

Andrew Sears (AS) studied Art History at the University of California in Berkeley. He provided curatorial support for the exhibition Beyond Compare: Art from Africa in the Bode-Museum, Bode-Museum, Berlin (2017–2019) and since 2021 has been a research assistant in the Department of Premodern Art at the Universität Bern.

Hans-Ulrich Kessler (HUK) is a research associate at the Bode-Museum, Staatliche Museen zu Berlin, where he has been responsible for northern European sculpture from c.1520–1800 since 2003. He has published extensively on Italian and northern European sculpture. He has also organised various exhibitions, including Caravaggio in Prussia (Rome and Berlin, 2001), John Flaxman and the Renaissance (Berlin, 2009) and Andreas Schlüter and Baroque Berlin (Berlin, 2014).

IMAGE CREDITS

Cover:
© Staatliche Museen zu Berlin, Skulpturensammlung and Museum für Byzantinische Kunst, Ethnologisches Museum, Museum für Asiatische Kunst

Backcover:
© Staatliche Museen zu Berlin, Skulpturensammlung and Museum für Byzantinische Kunst, Ethnologisches Museum, Museum für Asiatische Kunst

p. 6:
© Stiftung Humboldt Forum im Berliner Schloss / Staatliche Museen zu Berlin, Skulpturensammlung and Museum für Byzantinische Kunst, Ethnologisches Museum. Photo: Andreas König

p. 8 above left:
© Staatliche Museen zu Berlin, Ethnologisches Museum / Stiftung Humboldt Forum im Berliner Schloss. Digital reproduction: Jester Blank GbR

p. 8 above right:
© Staatliche Museen zu Berlin, Skulpturensammlung and Museum für Byzantinische Kunst. Photo: Antje Voigt

p. 8 below:
bpk / Ethnologisches Museum, SMB / Waltraut Schneider-Schütz

p. 11 above:
© Staatliche Museen zu Berlin, Ethnologisches Museum

p. 11 below:
bpk / Zentralarchiv, SMB

p. 12:
© Staatliche Museen zu Berlin, Zentralarchiv

p. 14:
bpk / Staatsbibliothek zu Berlin / F. Albert Schwartz

p. 16:
© Stiftung Humboldt Forum im Berliner Schloss / Staatliche Museen zu Berlin, Skulpturensammlung and Museum für Byzantinische Kunst, Museum für Asiatische Kunst. Photo: Andreas König

p. 18:
© Stiftung Humboldt Forum im Berliner Schloss / Staatliche Museen zu Berlin, Skulpturensammlung and Museum für Byzantinische Kunst, Ethnologisches Museum, Museum für Asiatische Kunst. Photo: Andreas König

pp. 20, 21:
bpk / Ethnologisches Museum, SMB / Waltraut Schneider-Schütz

p. 22 above:
© Staatliche Museen zu Berlin, Ethnologisches Museum / Stiftung Humboldt Forum im Berliner Schloss. Digital reproduction: Jester Blank GbRn

p. 22 below:
bpk / Ethnologisches Museum, SMB / Martin Franken

p. 23:
© Staatliche Museen zu Berlin, Skulpturensammlung and Museum für Byzantinische Kunst. Photo: Antje Voigt

p. 24:
© Stiftung Humboldt Forum im Berliner Schloss / Staatliche Museen zu Berlin, Ethnologisches Museum, Museum für Asiatische Kunst, Skulpturensammlung and Museum für Byzantinische Kunst. Photo: Andreas König

p. 26:
bpk / Ethnologisches Museum, SMB / Martin Franken

p. 27 above:
© Staatliche Museen zu Berlin, Ethnologisches Museum. Photo: Martin Franken

p. 27 below:
© Christian Lutz

p. 28:
© Staatliche Museen zu Berlin, Ethnologisches Museum. Photo: Claudia Obrocki

p. 29:
© Rubin Museum of Art, C2006.66.28 (HAR813)

pp. 30, 31:
© Staatliche Museen zu Berlin, Skulpturensammlung and Museum für Byzantinische Kunst. Photo: Antje Voigt

p. 32:
© Stiftung Humboldt Forum im Berliner Schloss / Staatliche Museen zu Berlin, Skulpturensammlung and Museum für Byzantinische Kunst, Museum für Asiatische Kunst, Ethnologisches Museum. Photo: Andreas König

p. 34 above:
© Staatliche Museen zu Berlin, Skulpturensammlung and Museum für Byzantinische Kunst. Photo: Antje Voigt

p. 34 below:
© The Metropolitan Museum of Art, New York

p. 35 above:
© Staatliche Museen zu Berlin, Skulpturensammlung and Museum für Byzantinische Kunst. Photo: Antje Voigt

p. 35 below:
imago

p. 36:
© Staatliche Museen zu Berlin, Skulpturensammlung and Museum für Byzantinische Kunst. Photo: Antje Voigt

p. 37 above:
© Staatliche Museen zu Berlin, Ethnologisches Museum. Photo: Claudia Obrocki

p. 37 middle and below:
© Henriette Lavaulx-Vrécourt

p. 38:
© Staatliche Museen zu Berlin, Ethnologisches Museum. Photo: Claudia Obrocki

p. 39:
© Heinrich Pöll

p. 40:
© Ross Archive of African Images (RAAI)

p. 41:
bpk / Ethnologisches Museum, SMB / Martin Franken

pp. 42 and 43:
bpk / Ethnologisches Museum, SMB

p. 44:
© Stiftung Humboldt Forum im Berliner Schloss / Staatliche Museen zu Berlin, Ethnologisches Museum, Museum für Asiatische Kunst. Photo: Andreas König

p. 46:
© Staatliche Museen zu Berlin, Ethnologisches Museum. Photo: Martin Franken

p. 47:
bpk / Ethnologisches Museum, SMB / Erik Hesmerg

p. 48:
bpk / Ethnologisches Museum, SMB

COLOPHON

Published by the Stiftung Humboldt Forum im Berliner Schloss

This book is published in connection with the exhibition ***ANCESTORS, GODDESSES AND HEROES: SCULPTURES FROM ASIA, AFRICA AND EUROPE*** at the Humboldt Forum Berlin, 2022–2023

An exhibition by the Stiftung Humboldt Forum im Berliner Schloss in cooperation with the Ethnologisches Museum and the Skulpturensammlung and Museum für Byzantinische Kunst in the Staatliche Museen zu Berlin – Preußischer Kulturbesitz

Exhibition curatorial team:
Julien Chapuis, Henriette Lavaulx-Vrécourt, Barbara Lenz, Bernadette Bröskamp, Tanja-Bianca Schmidt, with expert advice by Jonathan Fine and Paola Ivanov

Exhibition project team:
Nathalie Küchen, Constanze Wicke, Saro Gorgis, Noelle von Galen, Anne Jänichen, Johanna Kapp, Maria Mazgaj, Friedrun Portele-Anyangbe, Maike Voelkel

Head of exhibition department:
Anke Daemgen

Managing director of programme and projects:
Lavinia Frey

Exhibition design and graphics:
Günter Krüger (scala), Antonia Neubacher

Lenders:
• Ethnologisches Museum, Staatliche Museen zu Berlin
• Skulpturensammlung und Museum für Byzantinische Kunst, Staatliche Museen zu Berlin

The Stiftung Humboldt Forum sincerely thanks for their professional assistance and support: the authors, the lenders, Hilary Balu, Babette Buller, Michael Brandt, Yiqiang Cao, Shi Dengjue, Cäcilia Fluck, Ulrike Göken-Huismann, Sven Haase, Barbara Haussmann, Christine Howald, Michaela Humborg, Nina Kadri, Hans-Ulrich Kessler, Sheraz Khan, Alisa LaGamma, Tatjana Lamfried, Jeong-hee Lee-Kalisch, Wenhua Luo, Gabriele Mietke, Tanja Milewsky, Ugochukwu-Smooth C. Nzewi, Ulrike Rau, Andrew Sears, Ulrike Uhlig, Hui Wang, Kristin Weber-Sinn, Xuansu Zhang

We are also grateful to the staff of the Stiftung Humboldt Forum im Berliner Schloss, the Ethnologisches Museum and the Skulpturensammlung and Museum für Byzantinische Kunst in the Staatliche Museen zu Berlin and all those not named here who contributed to the success of this project.

Concept/Publication project direction:
Nathalie Küchen, Susanne Müller-Wolff

Authors:
Bernadette Bröskamp (BB), Julien Chapuis (JC), Cäcilia Fluck (CF), Hans-Ulrich Kessler (HK), Nathalie Küchen (NK), Barbara Lenz (BL), Tanja-Bianca Schmidt (TS), Andrew Sears (AS), with the help of Jonathan Fine (JF), Paola Ivanov (PI) and Henriette Lavaulx-Vrécourt (HLV)

Copyediting:
Tanja-Bianca Schmidt

Picture editing:
Bernadette Bröskamp, Saro Gorgis, Henriette Lavaulx-Vrécourt, Tanja-Bianca Schmidt, Barbara Martinkat

© 2023 Stiftung Humboldt Forum im Berliner Schloss, Schloßplatz, 10178 Berlin, and Deutscher Kunstverlag GmbH Berlin München

www.humboldtforum.org

Supported by the Federal Government Commissioner for Culture and the Media according to a resolution of the German Federal Parliament

External links contained in the text could be reviewed only up to the publication date. The issuer and publisher have had no influence on later changes and can therefore accept no liability.

The Deutsche Nationalbibliothek lists this publication in the Deutsche Nationalbibliografie; detailed bibliographic data are available on the Internet at http://dnb.dnb.de.

Publishing:
Deutscher Kunstverlag GmbH
Berlin München, Lützowstraße 33
10785 Berlin
www.deutscherkunstverlag.de

Part of Walter de Gruyter GmbH
Berlin Boston
www.degruyter.com

Project management:
Luzie Diekmann
(Deutscher Kunstverlag)

Production management:
Jens Lindenhain
(Deutscher Kunstverlag)

Translation from German into English:
Bronwen Saunders

Copyediting:
Aaron Bogart

Layout and typesetting:
e o t. Berlin

Image processing:
Bild1Druck GmbH, Berlin

Printing and binding:
Grafisches Centrum Cuno GmbH & Co. KG, Calbe (Saale)

Printed in Germany
All rights reserved.

ISBN 978-3-422-99090-6

Die Beauftragte der Bundesregierung für Kultur und Medien